WILLOW CREEK MEMOIRS

REVIESED SECOND EDITION PUBLISHED 8/29/2018

kindle direct publishing

Contents

kindle direct publishing

Chapters

Chapters

Epilogue

kindle | direct
publishing

Chapter 1 *The Beginning*

Growing up in the small sleepy town of Willow Creek in the 1950's was quite different than the way things are today. After WW 2 soldiers came home eagerly hoping to return to the lives they had been forced to leave behind as they marched off to war. Some soldiers were looking forward to rejoining their wives and families. Others eager to rekindle relation-ships with girlfriends they had been forced to leave behind. Most were hoping to come back to their old jobs or try to start entirely new careers. All these young men wanted was to get back to the normal ways of life.

What had once been small dairy farms, hay fields and shady wooded plots were slowly being developed in order to provide housing for the returning soldiers and their new families. As these tracks of affordable homes grew, so did the town of Willow Creek. It was the kind of place where almost everyone who lived in the area knew their neighbors by first name. Most of the men worked during the day which left the women at home to watch the kids, cook meals and care for the house.

Each evening there was a ritual when my father returned from work to mix a shaker filled with gin or vodka and just a splash of vermouth he called a Dry Martini or a mixture of whiskey, vermouth and bitters they called the Manhattan. Ashtrays could be found on almost every table and there was a never-ending cloud of tobacco smoke. L&M, Pall Mall, Camel and Lucky Strike were just a few of the brands I can recall.

As the German patrols had been scouring the area of the small town looking for the two American soldiers, who had been hiding behind this six-foot-high picketed stockade fence for several hours. Both men were ready for the inevitable battle that was about to take place. There was a squealing sound of the German tank tread as it made its way towards their position. Pulling the ring which held the detonator pin in their hand grenades, they flipped them over the fence. There was a deafening blast and when the smoke cleared the tank moved no more. Rifles in hand the soldiers quickly moved to a position on higher ground. Opening fire, the two soldiers took out the rest of the German patrol. Both men new they had succeeded and would live to fight another day.

John turned to his trusted sidekick and inquired "what are you having for supper?". "Leftovers" the soldier replied. "You?". I don't know, I'll go in and ask. Both boys put their sticks down on the picnic table.

These weapons had served them well on this day. If you grew up in the 1950's you would know that sticks were the all-purpose weapons of choice. Today rifles, tomorrow they could be swords, spears, ray-guns or any other weapon necessary to vanquish the evils in the universe. It had become a common practice to have a friend over for dinner. So, after inquiring and comparing our mothers' dinner menus, we would both decide at which house to partake of supper, if our parents permitted. That is, if we were home from our daily adventures in time for supper. Being late for dinner was something that did happen far too often. I will never forget the angered look on my parents' face at those times that I entered the house late.

Mom, dad and sister were all seated at the dining

room table waiting for my arrival. My father would not say a word but the look on his face told me I was in big trouble. Often, they would send me to my room without supper or even worse, I might be grounded. When these late for supper occurrences started to become much to common, my mother being the self-appointed peacemaker of the family knew she would have to come up with a way to get me home at the proper time.

I'm not sure where she obtained the whistle. Maybe from one of the local police officers that would frequently cruise the neighborhood. All I can remember is it that it was so loud you could hear it all the way across town. Three bursts meant it was time to get back to the house for supper. It didn't take long before the parents of all the kids in the neighborhood were told to get home when they heard Mrs. S's whistle.

In these times sharing was popular among neighbors. New homemakers would often find themselves in need of a pot, pan or a recipe that they would borrow from a neighbor. It would give my mother and her friends a chance to catch up on all the local gossip. When German Measles or Chickenpox showed up, our folks would send us to play with the kid that was infected. No quarantine in those days. We all were sick together. Yep, that is what sharing was all about.

Anyway, let's get back to supper. John's mom got on the phone with my mom to make sure it would be okay for me to have dinner with them. I believe the conversation may have gone something like this. "Hi Helen! just wanted to check in with you and make sure it would be okay for Alan to have supper with us?" "Sure, that would be fine" my mom replied. "What are you having? He can be a bit finicky!" "Meat loaf" answered John's mom. My mother laughed, "He won't eat it! Two things we can't get him to eat, tomatoes and meat loaf!"

The reason I hated tomatoes was because there was a wild plant that grew in the area around my house. The berry on this plant looked very much like a small miniature tomato. For some dumb reason I decided to eat some. I believe they call the plant nightshade. I'm thinking it was very poisonous and fortunately for me the overpowering taste of tomato started to gag me, and I spit out the berries. More than sixty years have passed and to this day I still can't eat a raw tomato. Meatloaf on the other hand was something that for some reason I just didn't like the looks of back then. This stay over at my friend's house could be a bit of a problem unless my mom could come up with plan! Now in these early days of my youth the story of Davy Crockett had taken the country by storm. We all were wearing coonskin caps and fringed pants that looked like buckskin. Davy and George Russell were my greatest heroes. I believed that anything these mountain men would do had to be good. After all they both lived by the motto "Be sure you're right and then go ahead". So, both our moms put their heads together and came up with a plan. "Let's tell the boys were having bobcat from one of Davy's original recipes." I guess back then I was pretty darn gullible, because I took the bait hook, line and sinker. "bobcat!" I could barely contain myself. I was sure Davy would approve of such a meal. After all, bear, bobcat and any of the other wild critters of the forest would be considered fine table fare for my heroes. That evening we both took our places at the table as Johnny's mom placed the platter in front of us. Turning to John I exclaimed "Hey I thought you said we were having bobcat!" His mom quickly jumped in to the conversation, "Cooked up just the way Davy said."

That day I ate two plate-full of bobcat and strange as it may seem, from then on, I no longer turned up my nose at meat loaf. My coonskin cap and buckskins are now only a dusty memory from when I was a young boy. Yet, if you spend any time visiting a mountain lake or stream or walking the winding path of a whitetail deer, you might come across an old gray-haired man who is still following the trails that Davy and George Russell blazed in my mind as a young boy so many years ago.

The Neighborhood Supper Time Whistle Blower

My Mom

Chapter 2 *Prejudice*

Working for a living was something that had been instilled in me very early in my youth. My first job was to use the old push mower to cut the grass. As I recall the faster you pushed the mower the better the blades cut. This was OK with me because I would finish my chore very quickly. I believe for this weekly labor I would receive an allowance of $1.50. Not much of a paycheck! Still it was enough to get a root beer or an egg cream at the Chocolate Shop in town and still have money left over for some penny candy. One of my favorites was called Fireball. They were red colored round balls the same size as a bigeye or shooter marble. Dyed red and flavored with hot cinnamon, too hard to chew, you would have to suck on these marbles like candies until they got small enough to crunch. They would last for a long time in your mouth and would leave you with a bright red tongue when you were finished. The other thing I liked was pumpkin seeds. I think they cost around 5 cents a box. The seeds were heavily encased in a salt paste and you would suck on them until the salt was gone before eating the seed. This made a box of them almost as long lasting as the Fireballs.

Several stores down from the Chocolate Shop was the Five & Ten Cent store. This was my other favorite place to spend my hard-earned cash. The store was filled with small inexpensive toys. Jacks, cap-guns, puzzles and my favorite, small pocket knives. These knives were no more than an inch long and the blade was dull, but because I was still too young to have a real knife, these would fit the bill. Trouble came the day I finally purchased one.

Sitting in the living room at home I was fiddling around with the small knife when my father entered the room. He had a strange look on his face as he asked to see my knife. I had believed my parents would not be concerned about such a small dull toy. Not realizing why, he was looking so closely I blurted out "Dad it's not even sharp!" That was when he spoke. "Alan! That's not what I'm looking at. Can you see the stamp on the blade?" he asked. "Made in Japan. You are not to bring home any toy that is stamped Japan."

It seems after WW 2 the Japanese were struggling to get back into the import-export trade. What was coming into the U.S.A. from Japan were these small inexpensive toys that the kids my age could afford and were eager to obtain. At this time my father still carried the scars of war. "Our house will never support the Japs," he scolded.

This was the first time I had seen what racial prejudice might look like and unfortunately it wouldn't be the last. I must say that at the time his feelings on this matter were completely understandable and common.

When word got around about these cheap toys, the sales suddenly dropped off drastically. The Japanese changed the name of one of their towns to USA. Products were now marked "Made in USA. "These Japs were pretty tricky devils. They pulled this off for a while until word got around the neighborhoods. For some time after, I wasn't allowed to bring home any cheap toys no matter what the stamping.

In these early days the town of Willow Creek was

made up of two basic religious groups. WASP \ White Anglo-Saxon Protestant and Roman Catholics. So, in other words Willow Creek was an all-white community. As kids we had no idea about any kind of racial bias or even thought about our towns ethnic makeup, until the day my dad told me, "Get into the car. I want to show you something!"

We drove several blocks from the house before he pulled over to the curb. "You see that house?" he pointed. "Black people bought it. You keep an eye on that place because it won't take long for them to trash it! This is a bad thing for our neighborhood." I had no idea what my dad was talking about, but in these times, we were taught to always listen to what our fathers were telling us. "Just ask Dad" was what the ads told us.

It was during this time that I had gotten my first paper route. It ran past the house my father had taken me to see. Keeping a close eye on this home as I delivered my newspapers, this strange thing he told me about these people made no sense to me. Yet believing that my father must know something about this matter, I would bring him back a weekly report on the condition of the house.

This property was very well maintained and each time I returned with another positive report, dad would simply give me a "Humph" in response. Convinced that what I had been told was true, I started to inquire with some of the neighbors. This is when I found out that the man in the house was a well-known doctor who had landscapers to care for the house and grounds. Also, that the whole family were actually very nice people. This was one of the few times my father ever told me something which I believe was totally wrong. The thing I learned from this was to never judge people by race or religion. Everyone bears the weight of his own behavior regardless of his or her faith or the color of their skin.

I must tell you all who may be reading this that my father's thoughts changed on these matters with time. I believe much of what he was telling me was passed down from his father to him. I was lucky that my first encounter went the way it did or else I might have accepted what I was told as fact.

The 1960's would bring many of these racial and religious beliefs to the foreground. Eventually these tensions would come to an exploding point, but for the time being it's just the way things were.

Chapter 3 *Punishments*

Getting in trouble was something I had become a professional at as a young boy. As I may have previously mentioned, there were various grades of punishment a young fella would have to endure as he was growing up in Willow Creek. If you arrived home late for supper you were sent to your room with an empty stomach. Being grounded was another method used, but at least in my case this was not implemented often. The reason being it was more of a punishment for my mom than it was for me. Making me stay around the house all day would eventually drive her crazy. You see my sister and I would fight about almost anything one could imagine.

During the days of inclement weather, I believe mom would occasionally put a serious dent in a bottle of Beef-eater stowed in the fridge just trying to cope with our bickering. Another thing they tried was taking away my allowance. This was not effective punishment since from an early age I always attempted to find some way to generate income for myself, delivering papers, shoveling driveways and such. My parents soon learned that this method was somewhat ineffective. Removing TV privileges was also used for a time, but it never really bothered me much and left me more time to quarrel with my sister. The only form of punishment that I received that worked was what folks called corporal; It was delivered using a large wooden spoon. Oh, how I feared the pain that spoon could deliver to my backside. Wrong behavior was never ignored. If you were disrespectful to an adult or your parents, your backside would be reddened by that spoon. Although I was no angel when it came to getting in trouble, the simple moral teaching of right and wrong was drummed into me from an early age. So even when I crossed over the line and found myself in trouble there was never any doubt that what I was doing was wrong. Our parents never made excuses for bad behavior, and punishment was always dealt out quickly. One incident I can recall had to do with an older boy from the neighborhood. For some reason which I never understood, he decided to bully me. Not physically but by use of threatening phone calls. I had become so upset that this guy was going to get me I was afraid to go to school. Finally, I couldn't stand the stress anymore and turned to my parents for help. One phone call was all it took.

The doorbell rang, and pure fear hit me when I saw that my tormentor was at the door. He was not alone. Standing next to him was his father. The man was holding his son's ear in a reverse bent position. He told the boy to apologize and warned him if he ever bothered me again he would break his hand.

I believe he meant every word of what he said. That was the last time I would ever have any trouble with that boy, but this story is not really about this incident. What I'm trying to show is how our parents taught us right from wrong. It seems to me that today parents tend to shelter their children, refusing to accept the fact that they are acting bad. "Not my son or daughter!" is heard much too often. Today the belief is to reward children for behaving good not to punish them when they are bad. It's my belief that good behavior should be expected from a child. Giving them rewards for these actions teaches them nothing. Everyone can't be a winner in real life. Its earned by hard work and perseverance.

As time went by, the wooden spoon finally broke and I laughed at the blows I received. But by then my moral fiber had been instilled and I understood right from wrong.

Chapter 4 *Always Too Young*

It's kind of odd the way time can play games with people. My own personal observation about this phenomenon makes me tend to place our lives into several distinct categories. The first of these I will refer to is the early stage.

During this part of life's journey, the future does not exist. What matters is our present need. If were hungry, food makes us content. Wet diaper when changed makes life good. There is no thought of tomorrow during this early time. Only things that fulfill our immediate needs have any meaning or importance at this stage of our development. Not long after this a change occurs as we start to wonder. "Why haven't they given me food yet? I don't like the way this stuff tastes! I think there is a monster in that closet!" We've now entered the next part of the cycle of life. This is when things suddenly start to become more complicated. As a boy growing up in a small town, for some reason I always found myself too young for just about everything I took an interest in. It seemed that no matter what the task the answer from my parents was always the same. "To young! Not old enough! When you're older!" blah blah blah. Jeff can stay out and play after dark! Johnny rides his bike to school! Butch watches that show every Saturday night! Why does it always seem like I'm the only one in Willow Creek that's never old enough?"

I can still recall the way things used to be at the place I worked. Remembering the words my boss would often say to the other workers or a customer. "Get the kid to sweep the floor. The kid will carry that for you." Always finding myself to be the new kid on the block or just a helper on the job site. Funny how when we are young, we find ourselves constantly wishing to be older. "Next year I'm going to be able to do this and that!" Never realizing that we're all constantly wishing our lives away. Soon enough we find ourselves toiling through the week just trying to get to Friday nights and the weekend. This hurry up process continues through a good part of life till suddenly one day we realize something has changed.

The people you work with start turning to you for advice. It appears we never have enough time in the day to finish. Not working becomes a problem because jobs keep piling up and as I used to say, "I'm going to need a vacation to recover from all the work I had to catch up on after my vacation!" This subtle change signals the beginning of the next part of life's journey. Now that I have found myself in the autumn season of my life I'm trying to find as much time as possible to stop and smell the roses. Although I've long since left that small town of my youth I often recall those early days when time seemed to never move fast enough I realize now that those slow-moving moments have now become special places in my memory. If I only I knew then what I have long since come to realize, some of the most precious moments in my life occurred during those days when time seemed to just stand still as I was growing up in Willow Creek.

Chapter 5 Self Defense

As a young boy most of my playmates were a year or two older for some reason. Being born in December made me what was called a late bloomer. Many of my school classmates were a year ahead and in those early days of growth and change this would often make a major difference. Also, being born so close to a major holiday made me always feel that for some reason my birthday was somehow nullified because of all the attention being given to Christmas. Not sure why I'm bringing this up at this time, but I think that all of you who are born under the sign of Sagittarius will be able to relate to what I'm saying.

Anyway, let's get back to where I was going when I started this conversation. The saying of the day was "Two is a party, three is a crowd." If I was playing with one of my friends, we could spend an entire afternoon together and never have a disagreement. The moment another friend joined the group trouble started. The two older boys of the group usually excluded me as I have previously mentioned. I hated being picked on and couldn't figure out which of the boys made me madder. The one I had been playing with or the one who had just joined the group. All I can remember was I was the one usually left out. Too often I would just go home, complaining to my parents about my friends' unkind behavior.

It was at this time my dad figured I needed a few lessons in self-defense. In these young days of my youth a black eye or what my father called a shiner was considered a rite of passage. Part of growing up in Willow Creek was learning to take some lumps. Boys would often settle their differences by squaring off with each other. There was no disgrace if you happened to be on the receiving end of a fist, if you stood up to the fight. A raw steak was given to the recipient which was held over the swollen eye. I was never quite sure if this accomplished anything. I always thought it would have been better to just eat the steak, being that in these early days I seemed to have a hollow leg and always found myself hungry.

Anyway, back to my self-defense training. We had a next-door neighbor who was a friend of my dad. He had been a Golden Glove champion boxer. My folks decided to send me over for boxing lessons. I spent several hours a day for a week or so learning the basics of the sport. He taught me how to properly plant my feet to maintain solid footing, setting my left fist in a blocking position to guard my face. "Plant your feet the way I've shown you and it will help give you maximum power to your punches! Also watch your opponent's eyes. If he is moving a lot, always watch for when he lifts his foot. As he does this he will not be able to throw a punch and his guard will be lowered. That's when you throw your punch!" These were just a few of the tips he taught me. Fighting was something I really didn't want anything to do with, however if my father wanted me to learn then I had no choice in the matter. Fighting was just not in my nature. In fact, the whole Idea made me kind of sick to my stomach. Never the less I did what my dad wanted.

Well that brings me to the day of reckoning. I had been playing with one of my friends when another friend came over and joined us. He was two years older than me. I thought he was a cool guy who was always dressed in the most stylish clothes. His hair was always perfectly combed, and he always kept his comb in his back pocket just in case the wind or something knocked a hair out of place. Being that he was several years older, I looked up to him as somewhat of a man of the world. I cannot recall what button he pushed that day that might have set me off. But it was like I have previously mentioned, two is a party and three is a crowd. He started making jokes about me and talking to my other friend purposely, so I couldn't hear what he was saying. On any other day I would probably have just gone home at that point, but today things were going to be different. Something started to boil up inside me. I'm not sure what the words where I used but I do remember that they were what you would call "fighting words." He started circling around me, every so often throwing an air jab or two. His fancy footwork was making me dizzy and I felt very confident that he was about to give me a serious shellacking. It was too late to back out now. I would just have to get my lumps.

Standing the way, I'd been taught, my left fist in a guard position, my right fist back close to my chest I waited to try to gauge the timing of my opponent's footwork. His eyes widened as he lifted his foot to take his next step. This was it, my time had come to fire off a shot. Punching as hard as I could I hit him square on the cheek. What happened next took me totally by surprise. My opponent started crying and proceeded to run into his house threatening to tell his mom. My father would be proud! I had stood my ground and had been victorious. This would not be the last time I would find myself squaring off with someone, and I would not always be so successful as I was in this first fight. A slightly crooked nose and a somewhat bothersome sinus condition have been lifelong reminders that it's probably much better to just walk away.

Chapter 6 *The Underground Railroad*

Not far from the border line that separates Willow Creek form one of its neighboring towns stands a Catholic church and a large parochial school. What I want to mention does not really have anything to do with these two buildings except that it marks the general location of a place that I often frequented as a boy. This place of importance for my friends and I could be found directly across the street. There was a grand old house set back from the road on a heavily wooded plot of land. It had what might be considered a somewhat scary appearance. Not that the building was rundown in any way. It was just that it was very old and showed its age. You see, the grounds could be dated all the way back to the early days of the American Revolution. Our founding fathers used the location as a rest stop for their travels and shelter for family during the revolution. It was also believed to have played an active part in what was to become known as the underground railroad, helping to hide runaway slaves that were trying to make their way to freedom.

As young boys we had heard a rumor that there could be secret passages in or around that old house. That's what we wanted to find! We would search and search the grounds always keeping a close watch for the two large dogs that guarded the old house. These guard dogs were rumored to be extremely vicious an if they were out we did not want to get anywhere near them. Two old women lived in the house. It was said that they were direct ancestors of the estate's original owners. They were not known to be any friendlier than the pets that guarded that old house. For that reason, we kept away when they were about.

Railroad tracks ran past the back of the old house and beyond that was a pond we fished from time to time. It came to pass one day as we headed through the woods across the tracks that we spotted the tunnel. It was closed off with old iron bars that were beginning to rust away just enough so that we were able to squeeze through. The walls were made of large sandstone blocks placed one on top of the other to form the square mouth of the tunnel. This must be it! We've found it! The entrance to the underground railroad. Our next move was to go back to the house to get some rope and a flashlight. Oh, also a box of crackers because you just never know.

Upon our return the decision had to be made as to who was going to be the first to enter the tunnel. As it turned out we went in together, determined but also very nervous as to what we might encounter. About ten feet or so inside things suddenly changed. The square sandstone block turned to a concrete storm drain. We were disappointed about this change in the construction of the tunnel, although I do believe the original ten feet may have existed from old times. The rest was replaced for modern drainage issues.

We continued to crawl for roughly a quarter mile till we came to a daylight opening above us. We had reached the main road directly across from the church. It was fun waiting for cars to pass so we could pop our arms up out of the sewer drain and wave. Must have been a shock to quite a few drivers that day.

Tunnel crawling managed to keep us busy for a week or so till we became bored and decided to find a new adventure. On the last day as we were heading across the yard past the old mansion, a woman called out to us from the back of the house. Nervously we made our approach maintaining a close eye out for the two watch dogs that guarded the house. The two ladies informed us that they had just baked cookies and offered us some. They introduced themselves as members of the Rosencrantz family, the original owners of the estate. We asked them if the tunnel was part of the underground railroad and they told us no, that the house had a secret room that was built just for that purpose. We also learned that they only had one dog and he would just run back and forth from the front to the back of the house causing folks to believe that there were two. Just a note, the dog was in fact friendly. The ladies told us that they lived in only a small part of the house. The rest of the rooms had been left just as they were back in the 1800's. It was their plan to donate the property to the state after their passing. The building has since become a museum.

The Hermitage

Chapter 7 *Dangerous Hobbies*

The railroad ran through the heart of Willow Creek. As young boys it was always a special place for my friends and I to spend hours walking there. For some reason we were always fascinated with the tracks. Maybe because they seemed to promise us an opportunity for great adventure. Or it could have been the excitement when we heard the distant whistle that would signal a warning of an approaching train.

These iron horses would rumble and clatter past us before continuing their long journey to distant places that we could only imagine. When we would hear the whistle of an approaching train, we would often place several coins on the center of the polished track rails. A penny would end up the size of a half dollar once the locomotive passed over it. I believe some of these flattened coins may still be up in my attic tucked safely away in a corner of the rafters in a small box, kept as a reminder of a time when I was young.

It was on one hot summer day that my friend Butch

and I were walking the rail past a switch back track. These switch tracks were places trains that were out of service or not currently needed could be safely stored. I'm not sure how Butch had become so knowledgeable about the railroad. Maybe his father or some other close family friend worked there, whichever way he seemed to know everything about the trains.

One piece of information he had acquired was of extreme interest to both of us. He had heard that the caboose, the last car on the train contained a red canister which was mounted on the wall by the back door. These canisters contained emergency flares and something else that we were both very interested in. My friend had learned that they also stowed warning charges in these red containers. They were wax coated squares measuring approximately three inches in size and about a half inch thick. Each had a strip of lead running through the center. This strip was designed to fasten the charge to the train rail. Compression was the detonator for these charges. They were to be fastened on the rail if there was a problem on the track. As another approaching train would run over the charge it would explode. Butch claimed that the bomb was equivalent to a quarter stick of dynamite. The blast could both be felt and heard by the conductor giving them warning time to slow down the train.

Now I must say at this point that what the two of us were doing was indeed wrong. But for some reason even though we knew better, my friends and I would have to stumble through many pitfalls of wrongdoing as we were growing up. Hopefully we would eventually get things right, but for the time being all we could think about was how we were going to set off those charges we had in our pockets. Butch had also mentioned that the trains carried larger explosive grenades. He believed they were stowed in a compartment somewhere under the train. These explosives were to be used to remove a tree or some other obstruction that had fallen onto the tracks. Now I believed Butch's knowledge on trains to be extremely credible, so the two of us spent a good hour searching. Fortunately, we could never locate where they were stowed. This story may have had a much different ending if we had succeeded. After failing to find the grenades we headed back to our development. Not far from our houses was an old hay field that had been cultivated by local farmers for many years.

There was a small graveyard at the top of the field. Some of the stones dating back to the early seventeen hundred. Most of the grave stones had fallen over long ago, but under close examination the names and dates could still be seen. At the bottom of the field was a wooded area and an old wagon road from days gone by. On the other side of the road was the swamp. This place was where I would spend many of my early days.

Anyway, let me get back to this story I've been telling you about. We had both decided this was a good place to set off the bombs. We decided to accomplish this by placing the charge on a boulder. We then picked up a second rock and dropped it on the explosive. It took several attempts before the stone hit the charge square enough to detonate. The explosion was so intense the boulder shattered and both of us were temporally deaf from the blast. Luckily neither of us were injured, although a later hearing loss could be attributed to these dumb actions.

After that we decided that we needed to figure out a safer way to set off these bombs. We placed the boulder at the base of a tree, then taking another stone we shimmied up the tree. Once we reached a safe height we dropped the stone. We finished blowing off the rest of the bombs in this manner and headed back home. often wonder how we survived all the crazy stuff we got into during our youth.

There was little known knowledge about toxic contamination in those days. I can remember how we used to bust open our grandparents' old hearing aid batteries which contained mercury. We would put the mercury in a small glass pill bottle and slip it into or pockets. Often, we would bring the bottle to school and play with it on our desk. If you put a small drop of quicksilver (another name for mercury) on a dime, it would instantly coat the entire surface of the coin making it shine as if it had just been minted. These coins were just put back into our pockets with the rest of our change. Today they would have to call in for a hazmat cleanup.

I used to help my dad apply creosote around the base of the house. It was great stuff for keeping ants away. After we applied the black sticky tar to the foundation, we would have to clean it off our hands. Washing off the tar was easily accomplished using a liquid my dad called Carbona. Straight gas also worked well as a hand cleaner, but you would smell like you had been working at a gas station all day.

Our vegetable gardens were rarely bothered by insects. The sprays which contained DDT were often applied. They worked so well they kept the garden bug free through the entire growing season. There were several types of garden sprays available for use, and they all contained some type of wonder chemical that could keep our vegetables and flowers pest free.

Many of the houses were sided with asbestos shingles. This tough material was known for its durable, weather resistant features, and used in commercial insulation and many other major applications, including the manufacturing of automotive brake pads. Every time one applied pressure to the brakes, a small amount of dust was ground from the brake pads. Ever stop to think about how much of this dust has gotten into our environment? All cars in the country had eight asbestos brake pads. If you were in hilly areas you could compound the amount of dust twenty or thirty times. Lead was commonly found in paints and other products. As a boy from time to time I would chew on a lead sinker. Lead sinkers used today are the same fishermen used for over a hundred years. If a fishing line gets snagged on the bottom of a lake, it deposits lead directly into the water source. In the 1950's lead was also commonly used in many of the toys we played with, such as toy soldiers. These toxics are just a few of the things we early Baby Boomers were exposed to that by today's standards should have put us in early graves. Maybe for some it did.

Chapter 8 *Picking Berries*

Willow Creek schools closed for the summer around the third week in June. My friend Ray and I got the idea to try and get a job to make some extra money. We both delivered Sunday newspapers, but that wasn't enough to cover what we had in mind. There was something both of us wanted to get our hands on before July. Fireworks! We had somehow learned that there was a place in New York City called Canal Street. We were told fireworks could often be purchased at this location which was in the Chinatown area. We started looking in the local paper for part time jobs.

We both spotted an ad from a local farm for pickers. Both of us knew where this farm was located because we often rode our bikes past their vegetable stand on our way to fish at a local pond. So, we climbed on our bikes and off we went. This was the peak of the strawberry season and the berries had to be harvested before they over ripened. They could only be picked in the early morning when it was relatively cool. Once the day heated up the strawberries were too soft to handle.

Our job interviews went well and we both agreed to start work at five o'clock the following morning. We settled on an hourly pay rate of one dollar and twenty-five cents an hour. Most of the pickers were paid by volume. The more crates one picked, the more money they made. Because we were new to this type of work the farmer advised us to take the hourly rate. Both of us started figuring how much money we could pocket before the fourth of July.

All the pickers were migrant workers. They traveled around the country following the harvest seasons of the various crops. On some of the larger farms, shack houses were provided for the workers. This was done because the farms grew more than one crop and sometimes harvests did not line up back to back. Rather than trying to find new workers when they were needed, the farmer would allow the pickers to stay in these small houses they were providing to ensure they had the workers they needed when the time was right. We found that most of these workers appeared to be in good spirits. They seemed to enjoy this Gypsy type of life, traveling from place to place across the country following seasons.

Our first day as pickers was about to begin. It was not long after sunrise that we all climbed into the back of a large wagon the farmer pulled with his tractor. This 'kinda reminded us of hayrides our parents would take us on in the fall. That trip out to the Strawberry fields was lots of fun. Especially after the farmer informed us that we could eat all the berries we wanted.

We could not believe we had found such a great job. At this point I will tell you something I never knew about strawberries. When you have a normal size serving all is good and they are wonderful. The difference is when you can eat all you want. Then it becomes and altogether different story. By the time we got up the following morning, the two of us looked exactly like the berries we had been picking and eating. You see, when you ingest too many strawberries you break out with an incredible rash or hives. One day was all it took to learn why they told us we could eat all we wanted. After that both of us were much more careful about the number of berries we consumed.

A strange thing the farmer did each morning as he drove us all out to the fields was to preach the gospel. I found this kind of odd but we all listened intently. This would soon become a life lesson which I will explain shortly.

When we arrived at the field we all climbed down from the wagon. The farmer would only stop at specific rows he wanted picked. Time was short, it wouldn't be long before the heat of the day would stop our work. All of us were working quickly, picking as many berries as we could while the fruit remained firm. Suddenly one of the pickers next to me yelled "duck, duck!" Not quite sure exactly what was happening, both of us put our heads down. That was when we were pelted with ripe berries. The man who had shouted out the warning to us pointed to another group of pickers several rows away. From then on, I was going to keep a close watch on that bunch. As I returned to picking, the warning yell came again. Once again, we put our heads down trying to prevent being splattered. It was too late! We both were hit again, and my anger started to get the best of me. Taking a hand full of berries, I heaved them back at the other group of pickers. There was one older man in this group that appeared to be their appointed leader. This man angrily began shouting back at the two of us.

This shocked me because they had started this berry fight. Things quieted down for a time, then suddenly once again came the warning shout. This time I started to duck but then quickly lifted my head back up in order to catch who the culprit was. This group I was watching seemed to all be hard at work. Their heads down focusing diligently on their picking. It was out of the corner of my eye that I caught the movement from the man next to us. It was just at that moment he yelled duck that I saw him throw the handful of fruit. The game was over, Ray and I moved away from this berry slinger. Both of us were mad at first but we had a good laugh after we calmed down. We were eager for that first day to end so we could wash the sticky berries from our hair. The week on our new job went well. All the pickers gathered at the vegetable stand to collect the week's pay. Each worker was handed an envelope except Ray and me. The farmer told us he felt we both needed a little more experience. "You boys work another week, and I'll see what I can pay you two!"

We were both floored by his statement. How could a man who seemed to almost be a preacher rip of two young boys? It took both our dads to get this man to pay up. The farmer gave the two of us the week's pay due us. We were both informed that we were not to report back to the farm on Monday because our employment had been terminated. Ray and I had both learned a valuable lesson. Never put full trust in someone based on outward appearances, or as the old saying goes "Beware of the Wolf in Sheep's Clothing

Chapter 9 *Canal Street*

Well, as I was telling you earlier both of us were hoping the money we made as pickers would have been enough to cover the cost of our fireworks. Instead, now we would have to dig into our own personal savings accounts. What I'm referring to was the top draw of my dresser. We both had managed to save enough money from our paper routes. By pooling it all together we managed to come up with around eighty bucks. So early the following morning we climbed up on our bikes and headed cross town to the train station.

It was a grand old building built 1886 as a service stop. The station stood in what could be considered the heart of Willow Creek. There was a hotel tavern adjacent to the station.

This old building had been vacated many years ago. After parking our bikes by the train station, we decided to try and get a look inside the hotel. Sneaking in through a broken window we found ourselves standing in the saloon. There was a long whiskey bar which probably doubled as a soda fountain back when the hotel was in operation. As I recall there were six or seven tables on the floor. I was always very inquisitive, so I peeked under the table closest to the bar. There tucked in a corner brace under the table were four cards. An Ace, King, Queen and Jack all Hearts if I recall correctly. Someone wasn't playing fair.

We carefully returned the cards to their secret hiding place. Only a ghost would now be able to use these cards on some unsuspecting spirit traveler. We found many pick cards behind the bar. For a small price a guest could purchase one or more of these cards. Using a toothpick, you would open five windows on the card trying to beat the poker hand at the top of the card. These pick cards were the precursor to the lottery scratch offs we play today. We both felt this old building was alive with spirits from an earlier time now long gone. Saying goodbye to the ghosts, we quickly climbed back out the window and headed back to the station. As we entered the station house, to our right we saw a double Dutch door. The bottom part of the door was closed and locked. The top half was open to expose a gray-haired man wearing thick horn-rimmed glasses. "Can I help you boys?" asked the man. We both walked up to the counter. Ray was the first to speak. "Sir, we need two round trip tickets to Chinatown." I cannot recall the details of our journey only that the next thing we knew was we were standing in New York City. We started asking people for directions. It didn't seem to take us very long before we found ourselves standing under a street sign which read CANAL ST. This is when we realized we had one problem that neither one of us had ever considered. Who is selling fireworks? So, sitting patiently on a green park bench we started watching people as they walked past us. What we were looking for was simply someone who looked like he may have something to sell. After an hour had past, there was still no sign of any one who fit the bill. We did notice one particular fella' who had been milling around by us for some time.

He was tall, standing close to six feet in height. His jet-black hair was greased back in what my mom called a duck's ass (DA). He was wearing wraparound sun-glasses. Finally, he approached us. "You guys need something?" he asked. "Yes!" we both answered in unison. "We want to buy Fireworks!"

"Well you boys have come to the right place! What kind do you want?" Ray told the guy we wanted a few mats of Black Cat. I added in a gross of cherry bombs or ash cans. Things seemed to be going well when our new contact suddenly became a bit nervous. He whispered that all three of us standing together was starting to look suspicious. He recommended that one of us go across the street and wait on another bench. As nervous as we both were, his suggestion seemed to make sense.

Ray crossed the street, sat on a bench and waited. I finished settling on the price and the guy told me he was going to throw in a bunch of rockets at no charge. This was going to be the best fourth ever. He pointed to a building across the street. "That's where we store them! I'll talk to my boss maybe because you guys are new customers he will throw in some more extra stuff. I can't

promise, but sometimes he will for a good new buyer."
The deal was almost done. He then suggested that I
count out the money. We had settled on a price of
seventy bucks. I counted it out for him and he re-
checked it. He told me his boss had to have the cash up
front. "I'll be back in around fifteen minutes or so!" he
said. I agreed and gave him the cash. We both watched
as he entered the building. Buy now I'm thinking you
must know where this is going. A half hour passed with
no sign of our guy with the fireworks. Ray came across
the street and we both sat together for another half hour
before we finally realized we had been conned. This
had turned out to be a time for learning for both of us.
Never put your trust in someone you don't know. Even
though he may preach like a minister from your church
or seem to be the coolest guy you've ever met, trust can
only be proven by actions not by appearances. This was
to be our second lesson at the school of hard knocks.

Train Station

Recently restored, it looks much nicer than it did back in the day.

Chapter 10 *All About the Game*

Baseball card collecting was very popular among the young people growing up in Willow Creek. Our bikes had baseball cards attached to each tire with clothespins. As we pedaled you could hear rat-tat-tat of the cards as they brushed against the spokes. On any given day you would see several of us standing in the street by a curb scaling cards.

Closest to the wall was what we called the game. If a card landed leaning upright against the curb it was usually considered a winner, unless an opponent could scale another card and knock it down. If someone's card landed close enough to the curb wall to touch it, this would also be a winner unless his opponent was able to cover that card with one of his own. By doing so he would cancel the card of his opponent. The winner takes all the cards that had been used in the game. There were several other games we also played with these cards. One which was my favorite was called 'match' or 'flip'. If someone had a card you wanted you would extend a challenge. "I'll flip 'ya for it." The idea of this game was to simply match your opponent's card. If their card landed face side up, so must yours to win the pot. After many hours of practice, I had become deadly at this game. On several occasions I challenged a friend to unlimited 'flip'. Each person was required to match heads or tails (picture side or back of the card.) You would continue flipping until someone failed to match. The winner got all the cards that had been thrown. Yes, with a little luck it was possible to double your card collection by winning one big game of 'flip' or 'match'.

The better cards in my collection were pasted into a collector's scrapbook. I still have a box of these glued cards. Some would now be valuable if they had not been glued. Now, they are nothing but old reminders of my youth. My dad had always been an avid baseball fan. He played semi-pro ball and the word around his home town was he was about to join the majors. Instead he enlisted in the army and went off to fight in the war. Many of his friends did in fact enter the pros, and whenever they came to New York they would call my dad. It was on one of these occasions that a friend of dad's who was a pitcher for the Cardinals as I recall, called and invited us to a double-header at Yankee Stadium. After the game he wanted to join us and take us out to dinner at the Waldorf Astoria.

The first game was what they called an 'old-timer's' game. Some of the most famous ball players in history took to the field that day to play what they referred to as an exhibition game. After that we watched the regular game. Dad's friend had invited us to come to the locker room after the game. This is when my story takes a strange turn. You see, as a young boy I had no interest in baseball whatsoever. I tried to play but a vision problem that I had from birth made it hard for me to catch the baseball. I had what was called a muscular imbalance in my eyes. In simple terms I saw double. Frustrated, I turned my interest to other sports. Fishing and hunting were what I felt I could do best and these sports have been with me my entire life. But for now, let's get back to that locker room.

Most fans would think that this was a chance of a

lifetime. For me, well let's just say I felt very uncomfortable. Strange indeed, I could have had an incredible collection of autographs and have had the chance to sit and talk with some of baseball's all-time greats. Instead I told my dad we should meet his friend at the car. Sorry dad! I know you tried. This would not be my father's last attempt to try and win me over to baseball. One summer morning he came in and woke me early. "Get up son and call your friend. You two take your bikes and go over to your friend Brian's house". He lived in the next town over from Willow Creek. "But dad", I said, "they're away for vacation!" He just smiled and told me, "Do what I say son!" So off we went. As we pulled into the long driveway we both noticed the large black limo. I will never forget the plate on that car, YB 8. We walked past the car and approached the side door of the house. I was just about to knock when I heard this deep growling voice. Never had I ever heard such a low baritone. Putting my fear aside I banged the door with my fist. A woman came to the kitchen door dressed in a full-length bathrobe. "Come on in!" she said, "We're just sitting down for breakfast." She had a warm, friendly smile which made us feel a little more comfortable as we went through the door. Sitting at the table were two boys, both around our age if my old memory serves me correctly. The nice lady said "Have a seat! Won't you two have some breakfast with us?" At that moment we froze. Sitting at the head of the table was an American icon. The man with the deep voice was no other than the famous baseball player Yogi Berra. Both my friend and I had been wondering why my dad had told us to make sure we took our glove and ball with us that day, now it all made sense.

We were in total shock, both of us standing by the table totally speechless. We extended our baseball mitts toward Yogi and neither of us spoke another word. He smiled as he signed our gloves, and after handing them back to us asked again if we would sit and have some breakfast. We still stood in silence, then in unison thanked him and turned for the door. Now I must tell you it was no accident that the Berra's were staying at my friend's home for the summer. Four houses down the road lived another famous man of baseball that I knew, but not in the way you would think. You see, the Saddle River where I fished as a boy cut past the back side of the home where the famous baseball player Ralph Houk lived. Each morning before he would go to work, he would come out of the porch on the side of his house and climb into a small swimming pool barely big enough for two people. If I was fishing that bend of the river he would often shout out and ask if they were biting. As far as I was concerned he was just a nice guy. I feel certain he arranged for the Berra's to stay at my friend's home that summer. How my father managed to set up our meeting with Yogi will remain a mystery. This would be the last time he would try to expose me to the sport. Although I have never forgotten this great experience, I have always felt bad that my interests never took to baseball. Instead my Dad and I started spending a great deal of time fishing together, casting lines on the water.

Chapter 11 *The Milkman*

One of the things I always looked forward to was the weekly visit from the milkman. This may sound a little strange, but he would always bring these great pastries along with the milk delivery. Also, he was extremely popular with all the young kids in the neighborhood. To us he was a real cowboy. His jacket was made of cowhide with fur intact. Cowboy hat and boots finished the look.

In those days westerns were very popular. Seems odd that we would wait for him to arrive with the milk just to talk and say hi. He was always friendly and eager to speak to us about his ranch. Something that he did for the local kids was cool. There was a pond on his property which he stocked with fish. Once a year he would put on a fishing contest for the local kids in the neighborhood. Now anyone who knew me would tell you that I was a Piscatorial Professional, born with fishing pole in hand. I was already making room for my trophy on the mantle and counting down the days to the derby, just knowing I was guaranteed to win.

The Saturday finally arrived, and I was ready, armed with my best fishing pole and tackle box. This was not going to be a contest, it was a shoe in for me. Fishing as hard as I could, my creel by the end of the day was exactly where I expected it to be. That big trophy was almost in my hand. There was only a minute or so left in the contest when something unexpected occurred.

As I looked across the pond I noticed a friend of mine standing at the edge of the water struggling with his fishing pole that appeared to be bent totally in half. He was not much of a fisherman, and when he started to walk backwards attempting to drag this monster fish up onto the bank I was sure it would get away. Well fate was not in my favor that day, for me or for that big old bass. We both ended up on the short end of the stick so to speak. The big fish would find its way to a platter as dinner at my friend's house and my trophy would sit on his mantle. After the derby my friend stopped by my house with his big trophy, setting it down on my bedroom dresser next to my smaller, second place one.

For a while I couldn't even make eye contact with him or look at that damn award. That's when he said something that hit me like a ton of bricks. He wanted to thank me for helping to teach him how to fish. "I set up my pole just the way you showed me. Bobber at two feet and the night crawler threaded onto the hook three times. I never catch anything! Just wanted to stop by and say thanks." Suddenly, losing didn't seem so bad. This fishing contest taught me how to deal with losing, humility, and the true value of friendship. Also, that a person's entire life can change in less than one second. These days twice a year we put on a fishing derby for the kids in our community. I now find myself watching carefully for the Piscatorial Professionals at the sign-up table and wondering what young kid who doesn't have a clue will win the prize for the biggest fish. Some of these kids have been coming back year after year determined to win that first-place trophy, and I'm sure some eventually will. It's my hope that these kids will learn something about life just the way I did fishing on the milkman's pond so many years ago.

Chapter 12 *A squirrel tale*

It was late summer when a major Hurricane blasted through Willow Creek. It flooded the streets of our neighborhood, uprooted trees and laid them flat across the lawns. After the storm had passed, I left the house to explore the damage the storm had inflicted on the neighborhood. I walked to the next block to see if my friend wanted to come along with me.

Outside his house was a large oak tree, it had survived the wrath of the hurricane, but the family of squirrels that had nested in the old tree had not done so well. Their nest had been ripped from its perch high in the limbs of that old tree and was now lying on the ground. Looking closer at the nest I noticed a slight movement coming from a balled-up mass of sticks and leaves. Carefully pulling the nest apart exposed a small baby squirrel maybe only three or four weeks old. Removing my shirt, I carefully wrapped it around the small animal and took him back to my house. We placed towels in a box on the porch and made a new home for my little orphaned friend.

That year Disney had been running a cartoon story about a squirrel named Perry, so that was what I would call my new pet. At first Perry did not trust me, heavy gloves were needed to handle the angry young squirrel. He would bite and snarl every time I attempted to pick him up to feed him. My mom had borrowed one of my sister's Betsy Wetsy baby doll bottles and we started bottle feeding the young squirrel. It wouldn't be long before Perry started to eat solid foods, seeds and crackers which soon became his regular diet.

I was able to discard the heavy gloves for Perry had finally gained trust in me. His favorite safe place would be for him to crawl inside my shirt. I guess to him it was security like his old nest. One day I was playing up the street, when my mom deciding it was time the squirrel should be returned to the wild, let Perry slip out the porch door. Well, it didn't take long for the young squirrel to find me. When I saw the animal's approach I was unsure, and I called out "Perry?". He quickly climbed up my pants leg and parked on my shoulder. From that day forward where I went, so did Perry.

I had learned that by pursing my lips and sucking inward I could make a sound that imitated the squirrel's call. Two such barks would tell Perry it was time to get up on my shoulder to safety. Perry would come with me when I collected for my paper route, and when we entered someone's house I would signal the squirrel to climb upon my shoulder. If I felt the homeowner might be nervous, I would let the squirrel slip into the safety of my shirt. One day I even took Perry to school for the day. We both spent many happy times together. Unfortunately, trouble was beginning to brew at home. You see, squirrels by nature like to gnaw.

When I wasn't with Perry, he would start to chew on the wood inside the porch trying to get out to find me. So, one night at dinner with Perry tucked safely in my shirt, my dad told me the squirrel had to go. With tears running down my cheeks I took the squirrel back to the oak tree where I had found him. The animal did not want to leave. I had to give the squirrel a smack and yell at him to get him to go up the tree. Totally beside myself I was forced to just turn and walk away. It would be several weeks before I would return to the oak tree to check on the squirrel. After I let out several calls, Perry came down the tree and perched on my shoulder, followed by another squirrel which seemed to maintain a safe distance from me. Perry had found a mate.

We had many visits that summer, and although Perry would scold his mate, she would never gain trust in me. One day as I stood at the base of the tree calling, there was no response. My friend came out of his house to inform me that Perry was dead. Apparently, the squirrel had tried to follow him into his house. His father not knowing about Perry, thought something was wrong and dispatched him with a shovel. My rage was more than I could contain. I was always taught to respect my elders, still I cursed the man in front of his company wishing he was dead. Looking back now, I can understand his actions. But at the time for me it was unforgivable.

My Friend Perry, May You Rest in Peace

Chapter 13 *Wrong Side of the Tracks*

As I have previously mentioned, the Erie railroad divided Willow Creek in two sections. Depending on which side you lived, when you crossed over the rails you could consider yourself on the other side of town or as some might refer, the wrong side of the track! Although actual geography is of little importance, this reference to tracks is.

You see, when I was growing up there was a certain group of kids that had a reputation for getting into more trouble than most. I could only guess at what the reasons were for their behavior. Possibly troubles at home or just a general rebellion against authority. Some just got mixed into the wrong crowd. Whatever the reason, the local police maintained close surveillance of this group. Many of these kids were what they called rebel greasers. Most would hang out at a house near the center of town. Some dropped out of school and many of the folks in town were in general agreement that this bunch would never amount to much of anything. Hence the reference, 'He's from the wrong side of the tracks!'

Strangely enough as time went by many of these dropouts would prove the town wrong. They would find jobs, get married and raise families. Some would become so successful as to rival or even surpass the highest achievers in town. To borrow an old saying "It's not where you've been, but where you're going that matters". The reason I bring this up is because to continue what I am about to tell you, requires a place for me to begin.

Most of what I write within these pages comes from what I can remember growing up in the town of Willow Creek so that's where I will start.

There were two brothers in town that I had made a casual acquaintance with. Both looked tough with DA haircuts and cigarettes rolled up in their t-shirt sleeve. One was loud and boisterous while the other seemed cooler and reserved. I believe both these boys were dropouts and could often be found at the residence I have previously mentioned. I can't recall the exact reason, but on one occasion I went to visit one of them. After leaving the house I was stopped by a local cop and asked what I was doing there. He then told me to stay clear of the place.

Anyway, that was all I needed to hear. I seemed to manage to get into enough trouble all on my own and surely didn't need anyone else to help. So, from that day forward other than a casual greeting on the street, I would manage to basically stay clear of this group for the rest of the time I was living in town. I'm not altogether sure how many years would pass before I would once again meet up with these two brothers. It was at least twenty years or more after I moved from Willow Creek that totally by coincidence we all settled in the same general area. The one brother was living on a small private lake which by an odd coincidence was the exact place my father took me to fish when I was just a boy.

The other was living just down the street from me. Sometimes it seems life is like a shoelace. Each time the lace passes through one of the boot eyelets, it draws itself tighter around your foot. As I have grown older I have become aware that much of my life seems somehow to come back full circle.

For well over twenty years I would work, hunt, and fish with these two brothers. Both had become my very close friends. When the one brother Greg, learned that I was temporarily out of work he was quick to offer me a construction job. Funny how I still can recall how at the end of each work day he would pull out a bottle of Jack Daniels from his freezer for us to celebrate completion of another successful day. Eventually a new job would take me in another direction, but both of us would remain as close friends even till this very day. Sadly, as time went by the other brother who I often hunted with fell prey to illness and eventually passed away. A farewell service was held at a small church near my home. I was amazed at all the folks that stood up and spoke about my friend. It seems he had been an active member of Alcoholics Anonymous since his early days in Willow Creek. Many of these people were recovering from drug and alcohol addiction. As each one stood to speak they all claimed the same thing. My friend was the only reason they were still alive. It seems that this so called 'loser' with his loud abrasive nature had managed to accomplish something in life of great importance. He saved lives! I felt compelled to say something about him at his service, but my words just seemed to fall short. Then something that had happened back when we hunted together came to mind. I remembered a much happier time when the two of us shared an adventure up on our mountain long before illness came and overtook my friend. These were my words for Tom:

The Nor'easter

It was late in the month of January. Folks on the mountain were preparing for a major snow storm. Most were thinking about 'cozying' up to a warm fire, possibly opening the pages of a good book. If you had any common sense at all, this was a day to be spent inside.

Unfortunately, my hunting partner Tom Miller and I never shared this type of attribute. This was the last day of the hunting season. Nothing could keep us off the mountain. We were battling with a bout of the flu which should have kept us both in bed. We were laughing as we started to walk up the old homesteader trail that ran off the back side of the mountain. Both of us must have been crazy heading out to the woods in our condition, but hunting is hunting. We stopped for a moment by the remains of an old stone foundation from an early settler's cabin. We couldn't help wondering how anyone could live in such a cramped space. The foot plan of the cabin was only twelve by twelve. We both agreed that life must have been very hard for these early pioneers. As we continued up the trail following alongside an old stone farm wall, Tom mentioned how it must have taken a lifetime to build all the walls that crisscross our mountain. Even with today's modern equipment it would be considered a major accomplishment. I wondered why no one ever figured out an easier way to mark off their land boundaries. Till this day, I still often think about how hard these early settlers worked and what they accomplished.

We were both heading for a special place where several of the old trails joined together forming what closely resembled a triangle. This place is notorious for big bucks. The land on one side runs off the top of the mountain through a large primal stand of pine. On the other side of the triangle was a wetland swamp. This place was the perfect home for the Whitetail deer.

Tom and I were both using climbing tree stands. We split the triangle between us. Picking out good climbing trees, we both locked our tree stands to their bases and stepped up onto the climber platform. Like giant inch-worms we pulled ourselves up to a height of around twenty-five feet above the forest floor. At this height we both had a clear view of each other and all the ground area around us.

Our scent could not be detected by approaching deer, nor would they see us. By the time we had reached the triangle snow had been falling for over an hour. It was building very rapidly. Wind had lost its direction blowing in spiraling circles. We were now being tossed around on our narrow tree stand platforms as if both of us were caught in a blender.

Just staying in the trees was hard enough, taking a shot at a deer would be quite another story. It wasn't long before we saw the buck approaching us from the pines. He could only be described as a horse with horns. Neither Tom nor I had ever seen such a large deer. Its rack extended around thirty inches off each side and rose up to huge double forks. What should have been tines were massive nubs, five on each side. The deer reminded me of the cartoon character Bullwinkle the Moose. Drawing my bow, I waited for the huge animal to come into shooting range.

Tom had been watching as this monster of a buck cautiously entered the triangle. He was holding on tightly to the tree as the wind attempted to shake him free from his perch. The deer was now forty-five yards from my tree. I was about to take my shot when the buck stepped behind a scrub cedar. It was only a matter of seconds, but the wait seemed like an eternity.

Tom nervously waited to hear the snap as my bow

was released. But the shot never came. Turning back toward the deep woods where it had originally come from, the buck quickly vanished back into the primal pines.

We were both totally frustrated. Tom tied his bow to a chord which he had attached to his stand, lowering it down till it hung just above the ground. The bow started to swing like the pendulum on an old German clock. This is when an eight-pointer approached Tom's tree. When it reached the base, it lifted its head and looked straight up. There was nothing he could do but wave at the buck before it wandered off. We used the same inch-worm method to climb back down out of our trees. The game was over for both of us. By now the snow was up to our knees. We decided it was time to start working our way back down off the mountain, splitting the trail between us, still hoping to come across a deer bedding in the pines along the way. The heavy snow was bending the pine branches down to a point of breaking. Ever circling winds would shake the snow free creating silver puffs in the forest like magic from a fairy tale. The snow drifts gave off a glowing blue light guiding our way down the trail. There was an old oak tree that had stood sentinel over the forest for well over a hundred years. This old soldier had finally tired of its position, letting the swirling winds take their course. The tree cracked, groaned and suddenly came down with a thundering crash. The old giant had finally come to rest. I could only hope that when it comes time and we are also laid to rest, it will be with as much honor and respect as that great old tree.

Tom and I left the forest without a deer that day, but I will always remember the rugged beauty on the mountain during that blizzard and the bond of friendship the two of us shared.

Early this morning I received a phone call. Tom had passed away. The winds had already started to blow and by daybreak the Nor'easter was releasing its wrath on our mountain. Rest in peace my old friend.

Chapter 14 *Bad Language*

The wind had been blowing hard across our mountain for several days. It was beginning to feel like the thick dark gray clouds and rain would never end. But as the weekend arrived so did the promise of clearing skies. I had become eager to get out of the cabin, so at the first sign that the wind was finally starting to calm I grabbed my fishing pole and headed down to the lake.

Waves that had been violently churning the surface waters for the past week were now gone and the lake looked like a sheet of glass. The surface was so still I could barely tell where it ended, and the evening sky began. Baiting my line for catfish I made a long cast and set the pole down leaving the bail open. Big catfish are notoriously hard runners and can steal a fishing pole from the bank in an instant. I was enjoying the calm, peaceful solitude of the mountain lake when I became aware of a group of young boys and girls that had gathered by one of the boat docks not far from where I was fishing. Their voices could be heard clearly, their words cutting through the quiet of the evening. The vocabulary they were using was based on four letter words or what you would call gutter language. Grating on my nerves more and more as each foul word spilled from their mouth, it didn't take long before I could no longer stand this rude disturbance.

Reeling in my line I had decided I would walk over and read them the riot act about the use of profanity in a public place. But a strange thing happened as I started to move toward their location. Something came into my mind from a time long past.

I started to recall a time when I was in the fourth or fifth grade walking home from school with one of my friends. We were accompanied by two girls from our class. I guess you could call them girlfriends, although the actual meaning was not completely clear to me at the time. We were all at the age of discovery of the opposite sex. Spin the bottle and making out were becoming the popular thing at our parties. I recall some of the girls in our class were developing faster than the rest and I believe some of these girls were quite proud of these sudden new developments.

It was not uncommon in these cases for young boys to try and cop a feel. Often by using a diversionary move such as being accidentally pushed. It's my hope that those who are reading this do not become offended by what I'm saying here, it's just the way I remember.

Anyway, as the four of us walked down the street we were all taking turns expelling four letter words. Or describing descriptive sexual acts and certain body parts and their functions. This could be considered strange behavior to say the least, and our actual understanding of the words we were using was weak at best. Never the less, I remembered those early days when we were coming of age. I'm sure anyone who could have heard those words that we were spouting would have been annoyed just as I had become that evening fishing. So, lifting my fishing pole I opened the bail and made another long cast. Realizing that as we get older we tend to become more and more critical of youth without remembering the things we did at that age so long ago.

These observations started me thinking about the different generations and the changes each went through. Often when you listen to older people like myself talking you will hear the statement, "Well, when I was young...!" or "It wasn't that way when I was a boy!" etc., etc.

Each generation goes through change, and the ones before will always have trouble dealing with what they are seeing as their children begin to spread their wings. In the twenty's it was the 'Flappers', forties were the war, fifties had grease, sixties had hippies and it keeps going on and on. Each older generation believing that the next new one may be totally lost. I guess what I'm trying to say is that although our parents may not agree with the ways of our youth and vice versa, history dictates that a certain measure of patience and understanding would be advisable. There is no way of knowing where these cycles of change will eventually lead us, but as we can see from our past it is inevitable that they are going to occur. Some may find disagree- ment with what I'm saying here and that's okay with me because it cements this phenomenon of progressive change of which I am speaking.

Not all people of an era embrace these changes of the newer generation. Some will hold on to the ways and teaching of their parents. There is nothing wrong with this although the newer group may wish to apply pressure to try and get everyone to agree with them. An example of this came into play in the 1960's. There was a saying "trust no one over thirty!" Although I did not always agree with my elders, this way of thinking in my opinion was ridiculous. Each generation should try to learn something from the other. Older groups speak from living experiences and new groups from current emotions in an ever-changing world. Both carry merit and if we could only learn to land somewhere in the middle we might all be a lot better off.

Chapter 15 *Bad Acting*

At the top of the street where my house was built lived a friend I will call John. He was tall as a beanpole and easily towered over most of the kids in the neighborhood. One day as I was walking past his house I happened to spot him and several of my other friends in his side yard. John was holding what appeared to be a hand-held movie camera. Several of my friends were dressed in their dads' army helmets and jackets. My curiosity immediately got the best of me. "Hey, what are you guys doing?" I asked. "Were making a war movie" they all chimed in at once. Looking on for a moment, I inquired "That's really keen, can I be in it?" "Sure!" John replied. So as fast as I could I ran home and grabbed my dad's old army jacket and helmet. We all did our best to reenact several battle scenes. One of the most interesting parts of John's movie I can recall was done with model army cars. It was accomplished by pushing them down a dirt mound simulating a crash. For what he had to work with, this footage looked neat. It seemed to me that I didn't personally get into much of that film. For some reason this bothered me much more than it should have. My obsessive nature, or the grasshopper effect as I often refer to it had crept up and bit me. Although at the time I didn't realize it a seed had already been planted that would come to haunt me later.

After a few years John moved to California and attended college for a career in the film industry. My family decided to take an extended summer vacation. Our plan was to travel cross country, California being the destination. John and his family were the last scheduled stop on our journey west before we headed back home to Willow Creek. We all had a wonderful time visiting together. I was very anxious to find out how John was doing with his film studies. Funny, but I still recall a large movie poster that was attached to his bedroom door. It was a picture of Clint Eastwood in one of his spaghetti westerns. Other than an occasional Christmas card or two, our families would basically lose track of each other as time passed by.

It would take twenty years or so before the seed that my friend had planted in my head would begin to grow. It wasn't till 1982 that I finally decided to sign up to attend a school for acting. After having photos taken and several mass mailings, I received my first casting call. I was to report to NBC studios in Brooklyn, NY for a soap opera called Texas. Over the next four years I managed to find extra work with three of the major networks NBC, CBS and ABC. I worked on a few movie sets including one with Robert Redford. Unfortunately, I never took this profession seriously. I refused to go to California, turned down a major villain role in a Grade B Movie that became a cult classic because I didn't like the contract. That film probably would have cemented my career. On one other occasion I was doing some thug work at NBC when another actor I knew asked if I wanted to work with him that evening as a bodyguard for a famous action movie star. It seemed that my friend played bad guys for the actor whenever he worked on films in the NYC area. He was being paid to eat in this restaurant that evening. We would both act as body-guards. It was a great chance for me to get to know this famous star who could possibly help kick-start my career. The press would do a story about how he was spotted eating at this establishment which would instantly attract customers. After giving it some thought, I decided coming back up to North Jersey late at night would be a real hassle, so I refused. These are just a few of the blown opportunities that came up on my plate. If you ever want to find out how to flush a career down the bowl, just call me. I'm an expert! Anyway, I would eventually get rid of my answering service in the city, take an honorary withdrawal from the acting guilds and put that career to rest.

Close to fifty years had gone by when I was lucky enough to get the opportunity to receive a visit from my old friend John. It seemed that his film career had taken him into the field of photo-journalism. He had been traveling all over the world for World Vision when he retired. It seemed to me that his life had been an incredible adventure. I think although he was retired, he was still not ready to settle down, so he got in a van and traveled all over the USA including my humble home. I'm not sure if my friend will ever really settle down. It's only my opinion, but I believe the lure of travel and adventure is in his blood, so at this time I would like to wish him a safe journey whatever road he may be on.

From my Acting Days

MARK MERRICK

SAG-AFTRA

Chapter 16 *Schneckenberg Stew*

It was the beginning of fall in the eighth year of my life. My dad informed me that the two of us had been invited to spend the weekend at a work friend's hunting camp. The plan was for us to get underway early Saturday morning, so we could arrive at the cabin before noon. I could barely sleep Friday night due to excitement about our adventure, so I slept most of the car ride to the camp due to the lack of rest I had gotten the night before. I remember waking as our car hit a pothole when my dad turned onto the semi-paved road that lead up the mountain to the hunting camp. Looking out my window at the dense dark green pine forest, I noticed a stream running along the side of the gravel road. Each time the road turned as we made our way toward the camp the stream followed. As the stream turned, it produced pools in which I was sure if any fish lived in the brook, these spots would be the place I would find them. When the cabin finally came into view, the stream suddenly took a sharp turn cutting across the road. An old wooden planked bridge clattered and shook as our car began to cross. I could no longer control my excitement and demanded that my dad stop the car.

Climbing out, I walked to the edge of the old bridge and gazed down into a deep pool. The water was crystal clear, and I could not believe the large number of trout that were sitting their facing up stream toward the rapids. Jumping back in the car I shouted, "Dad the stream is full of fish!" my father just smiled and told me "If Mr. Schneckenberg says it's OK, maybe you can fish after we get settled in at the camp." I could barely control myself as I exited the car by the cabin. After going through the formality of being introduced to my dad's friend Ed Schneckenberg, we unpacked the car and I suggested that maybe I could go down to the stream and catch enough trout for supper. Ed, as my dad called him, shook his head "Not tonight, I'm making you two something special. It's called Schneckenberg's Venison Stew. It's famous in these parts and there is no one who can make it better." I had never eaten deer and the thought excited my mountain man pioneering spirit. Davy Crockett would surely approve. 'Ed' as I will call him for the rest the story, suggested that we could fish for supper on Sunday, and I agreed wholeheartedly. He suggested that maybe we could do some shooting before supper. Now I had never fired a gun, and this was to be the highlight of this adventure. "Are we hunting?" I asked in excitement. Ed shook his head. "Nothing in season this time of year unless we see a varmint." Now being that I had never hunted prior to this day, I had no understanding of what constituted a varmint. However, I was going to keep a close watch in case some critter showed up that fit the bill. We spent the rest of the day 'plinking' beer cans, while I kept a close eye on the woods looking for those darn varmints whatever they were. Nothing that looked like what I would consider a varmint ever made an appearance that day. We did see several squirrels and some chipmunks which I started to take aim at before my dad stopped me. This was to be the beginning of my hunting career, although it would take two years before my dad finally would break down and buy me my first rifle for my birthday. Anyway, back to the stew. As the sun started to rest on the pines we all went back to the cabin. After Ed showed me how to clean his rifle, we sat down at the table with great expectation for his famous venison stew. He came out of the kitchen with a large pot containing the reputed masterpiece of culinary perfection. After prayers were said, he scooped each of us a large helping. Davy would never know what he was missing. I lifted a large spoonful to my anxious mouth closing my eyes in great anticipation. When the stew was finally delivered into my mouth, all hell broke loose. It was as salty as the sea and peppered in the same way. I glanced at my dad to see if he was having the same flavor experience that I was. Ed got up and went back to check on a pie he was making, and dad looked at me in shock. "Don't say anything," he whispered. "Try and finish your plate." Both of us struggled through that meal and thank goodness the pie wasn't bad. We would never figure out what happened to that stew or if the chef realized his mistake. If he did, he never let on.

From that day forward anytime, a meal went bad for some reason or another, dad and I would look at each other, smile and say 'Schneckenberg's Stew'.

Chapter 17 *Jingles and Bells*

Midsummer 1959 as best that I can recall. I will estimate the time to be somewhere between four and six o'clock in the afternoon, although in those days not much attention was ever given to the matter. The only thing that was necessary to be mindful of was supper time. In the earlier days of my growing up I would be called home in this manner: 'ALLL-ANNN! ALLL-ANNN!'

My mother's piercing call could shake the windows of our peaceful neighborhood. As I grew older, the distance from the house increased and it became necessary for her to come-up with a more effective method to rein me in for dinner. That was when the police whistle came into play. As time passed, that 'three blast call' would become universal for all the kids in the neighborhood. "When you hear that whistle, you head home!" During those hot days of summer there was another sound that ranked almost equal to my mom's call. It was recognizable from all the way up at the top end of our street. Sometimes it got our attention by the ringing sound of a bell. Other times it was heard as a simple jingle. Whichever sound caught our attention made little difference, as my friends and I lined up at the curb waiting for the white truck to make its approach. Pied Piper, Good Humor and Mr. Softy were the names that I remember. Ice cream was what we were waiting for. These trucks were all in fierce competition to be in the neighborhood when the kids were out on the street before dinner or just after. Otherwise their sales would be slim.

Good Humor was always my favorite, although I would make a purchase from any of these vendors. Timing was what made all the difference. One of our ice cream guys whom I will call Jerry, had become friends with all the kids on our street. He had come to the USA from another country. Sadly, I can no longer recall from where. He liked to tell us about how life was in his country and we all enjoyed his stories. He learned from our parents what the best time was for him to be in the neighborhood and had managed to develop a very good business. We were all happy for Jerry's success. One Saturday evening things took a bad turn for our friend.

He had stopped in front of our house and a large group of kids had lined up at the curb.

After Jerry completed his sales he got back in his white ice cream truck, waved and started to pull away. That's when we all suddenly heard the screams coming from under the front of the vehicle. It seems that just as Jerry started to pull away from the curb, one of my friend's little brother darted in front of the truck. He was so small it was impossible for the poor Ice cream man to see him.

In my mind I can still recall the sight as one of the parents pulled the little boy out from under the truck laying him on my front lawn. As it turned out the boy would survive. He did suffer some nerve damage to one eye. If there was any other injury, we did not know about it at the time.

No accusation of fault was ever made toward Jerry, although the poor man felt so personally guilty for the young boy's injuries, he quit the ice cream business. We saw him one more time when he stopped to inquire about the boy. I can only hope he was finally able to come to grips and find peace with what occurred that day. Sorry that I had to tell you about this but some things you just can't forget.

Chapter 18 *Sister Always Cries*

I can still recall the day they brought her home. There had been so much attention given to the preparation for my new sister's arrival, I was starting to feel like they had completely forgotten about me. Strange that I never questioned how my baby sister just suddenly arrived at our house. Thinking back, I can recall mom reading me this child's book on having a baby. She was attempting to fill in all the blank spots. You see my parents were not physically able to have children. We were both adopted at a very young age and have no recollection of life before our arrival in Willow Creek. Looking back now it's interesting how my folks arranged for both our arrivals to appear as if they were actual births. Personally, for me, this new intruder seemed to be more trouble than she was worth. Soon after her arrival my dad rented a lake cabin. I was still too young to recall its actual location. This was to be my first close exposure to this new person in my life. As I recall, gentle mist was falling through the pines that surrounded our cabin. I'm not exactly sure what had awakened me from my sleep as daybreak's glowing beams of light started to filter through the trees. Walking over to one of the cabin's window I was able to just catch a glimpse of mom pushing a carriage along the dirt road that lead away from our log cabin. Quickly slipping on my trousers, I exited the cabin running up the road to catch up with her. That's when I heard my sister's shrill screams.

Why would anyone want to deal with this? Maybe mom could just give her back, I thought. I turned to her and asked, "Mom why does Mary always cry?" As the years quickly passed by, we both suddenly found ourselves in high school. Mary was so smart she would constantly be on the honor roll. She was always getting A's and I was just wishing for a C. She was a cheerleader in school and was endowed with the good looks to go with it. It was my basic opinion that my sister had it made. One evening after we had finished supper, my sister and I had both gone upstairs to our rooms. I was staring out the window watching some of my friends playing in the court across the street from our house when I became aware that Mary was in her bedroom crying. "What's wrong sis?" I asked, standing by her door. "I'm ugly" she whimpered, "My ears are too big, I have no friends!" Walking into her room I sat down on the edge of her bed. "Listen, you have everything going for you. What you're crying about is crazy. You are so smart. If there was anyone that should worry about stuff like that, it would be me. As far as the way you look and the number of friends you have, any girl in school would love to look like you and be as popular. That's when something occurred to me. People often see themselves in a way that is far different from the way that others do. My sister's behavior confirmed this belief. I felt bad, but as she sat on the bed crying the only thing I could do was laugh. In the days to come she would graduate from college, become a school teacher helping special needs children, marry a good man and go on to live a full and wonderful life. And that's nothing to cry about sis.

My Sister and I

Chapter 19 *Two Houses*

In the 1950's, fields and forest still surrounded our home at Stuart Street in Willow Creek. If you walked out the front door, took a left turn and walked to the top of the hill you would be there. Only two homes existed on this large strip of land. They belonged to the original families of Dutch immigrants that settled in the area as far back as the 1600's. The first of these homes was a tall, stately, three floor block shaped building. The owners of this home were somewhat private folks. I would often walk down their long gravel drive that lead to the house to get to the woods. We never shared more than idle conversation, just waving or saying 'hi' as I made my way to the woods. At the time this house had been erected, it would have been considered the grandest of mansions. Three floors with fireplaces in every room. As time passed by the owners of this home decided to sell off their land. The home was put up for sale for one hundred dollars to anyone who would be willing to move it from its original location. I cannot recall if anyone ever attempted to try and accomplish this feat.

One day as I was cutting through the yard, Mrs. Lampe was working outside. I shouted out and told her that I was sorry she was leaving. That's when she asked if I would like to come in and see inside. Never having been in that grand old house, I jumped at the invitation. She proceeded to give me a grand tour from the basement to the top floor. The most interesting thing she showed me was a room up on the top floor. When she opened the door to the room I was warned to be careful. All the old plank floorboards had been removed exposing large round floor rafters. This is when my story gets interesting. She went on to tell me that the original Lampe was a wealthy ship builder. When he arrived in the Americas, he ordered his ship to be dismantled. The lumber was then transported to Willow Creek to build this grand old house. To me this must have been an incredible task.

The second home that I will mention was down the road a mile or so. An old apple tree marked the entrance. This old tree must have been at least a hundred years old. As a boy my friends and I spent many a day climbing in this grand old general. This was the Ackerman farm. This family owned much of the land that surrounded our neighborhood. Not far from the place we dug our forts and excavated the cow which I have previously mentioned, was a small cemetery up on a hill. Some of the early gravestones that could be read went back to the seventeen-hundreds. They all belonged to this family. These longtime residents of Willow Creek had two sisters that I knew. One was considerably older than me, the other was my friend. We would spend hours playing on that old farm. Climbing in the hayloft, chasing the feral cats that inhabited the barn, and just doing the things young people do. On this farm lived this creature that hated me as much as the old mule that used to chase me on the river bend. This nemeses of mine could not be intimidated. What I'm now speaking of is the biggest turkey I have ever seen. It was a regular practice for this evil bird to launch its attack whenever I came up the drive. If the girls saw my approach they would yell out the window, "Watch out Alan, that bird is out!" that told me to run like crazy for the barn. My greatest wish was that damn bird would someday end up as Thanksgiving dinner. Unfortunately to my knowledge this never happened.

My friend's grandfather was a rugged farmer. He had worked this old farm all his life and knew more about the area than anyone. I loved to talk with him about the history of the farmland and his early ancestors. He showed me the location of Indian grave sites out in the back fields which always fascinated me. All too soon this land was also sold off for housing tracks and all its history lost. But at least as I grew I was able to see and remember these things.

Chapter 20 *Santa*

Mary and I sat at the top of the stairs peering down into the living room. It was somewhere around ten o'clock when we had both 'snuck' out from our beds. The fireplace was giving off a warm red glow to the room from the few remaining embers that were still burning from the evening fire. Our folks never lit the fireplace except when we had guests over on special occasions. "You don't think the fire will keep him from coming, do you?" I asked. Mary shook her head, "He does it all the time." "Can you see any new packages under the tree? Maybe he already came!" I exclaimed. She replied, "It still looks the same as before we went to bed." We both agreed that It didn't look like there was anything in the stockings that were hanging from the mantle over the fireplace either. Also, the cookies and milk were still on the table untouched just the way we had left them for him. "Did you hear something?" I asked my sister. "What?" she asked. "I thought I just heard something on the roof!" I replied. Sitting in silence, we were gazing into the dimly lit room, both of us straining our ears to hear. After a while we both agreed it must have just been the wind.

Our furnace suddenly kicked on and the warm air that blew from the vent caused the lead tinsel that we had draped over the tree to dance giving off sparkling colors of silver, blue and gold. There was no doubt he was in the area, we both agreed. I had seen him earlier on the big red fire engine. He had stopped at the house to make sure we had been good and to ask what we were hoping to find under the tree. Mary had asked for this doll that cried and wet its pants. My wish was for a bike. Suddenly a thought came to both of us. Maybe he knows were up and he won't come. Fear suddenly came to us at the same time. Quickly we rushed back to our rooms and crawled under our warm blankets and fell off to sleep. So, as the saying goes "Merry Christmas to all and to all a goodnight."

Meeting with Santa

Chapter 21 *My Bike*

Bicycles were our main source of transportation as we were growing up in Willow Creek. It allowed us to get out of our local neighborhoods and explore or visit friends on the other side of town. One nearby larger town had a movie theater and our bikes gave us the opportunity to take in a matinee or shop in a larger department store we liked. Looking back now it's hard to believe some of the great distances we traveled exploring new places. Bikes were almost an extension of our bodies. I can't recall ever feeling fatigued from biking regardless of the distance we traveled but learning to use the bike was an altogether different story. My first bike came with a set of training wheels. These are small wheels that are fastened on each side of the rear tire preventing the bike from falling over. Although this attachment made the bike much slower and more cumbersome, it was my opinion it worked just fine. However, for some reason dad thought otherwise. On one Saturday as I took my bike from the garage, he confronted me with tools in hand. "It's time we remove those trainers" he exclaimed. "Dad you don't have to do that, they're fine. They don't bother me at all!" But my father would have none of that, those wheels were coming off. I can still recall how it took him hardly any time at all to remove them.

"Okay son climb up on your bike, I'll steady it for you!". Well it was a this point I decided not to take the bike after all. "Maybe I can just walk to Johnny's" I suggested. My father would have no part of what I was alluding to. "Get up on the bike Alan"! This time there was a change in the tone of my father's voice. Experience had taught me that when dad's voice sounded that way, he meant what he was saying. I knew it was best not to argue. With a great deal of hesitation, and dad steadying the handle bars, I climbed up on the bike. "Okay son start pedaling. I've got you!" At this point there was no turning back. As the bike started to build up speed, suddenly my father let go. 'This isn't bad'! I remember thinking to myself but as the bike started to slow down I started losing stability. The front wheel began to wobble so in panic I applied the foot brake. Then, everything went from bad to worse. The loss of my trainer wheels left nothing to keep the bike upright. As I locked down on the foot brakes, down fell the bike. My body hit the asphalt hard, scraping my elbow. Once I had recovered from the fall it was my suggestion we try this on another day. Nope, not going to happen, was what I suddenly began to realize. We repeated this same procedure so many times I lost count. There was no way I could escape from this torture. I started to realize that it was when I used the brake that all my problems started. So, when I felt I'd ridden far enough I started looking for a bush. Slowing down just enough to keep my balance I pointed the front wheel into the shrub. "Perfection!" I said to myself. Anyway, it sure beat crashing to the street. Now at least I had a system which could be used if I made sure I was out of sight of my father before implementing the procedure. Sadly, on one run I missed my bush leaving me no way to stop without falling to the blacktop. I was already all scraped up and decided that enough was enough. This was when I spotted one of my neighbors pulling into his driveway, parking his car. This was it! No time left to think about it, I was going in. I hit the side of my neighbor's car with a thud. He quickly climbed out of his car thinking he had somehow accidentally hit me. Leaving the bike where it fell, he packed me into the car and rushed me back to my house. Trying hard to convince the poor guy that I was OK made no difference. He was much more shook up than I was. Fortunately, there was no damage to his car, and after things calmed down and I assured him that I wasn't hurt, he left. Eventually dad was able to teach me how to use bike brakes and how to keep your balance by using your leg like a kickstand when you slowed down or came to a stop. Our neighbor's shrubs and car were finally safe from my assaults.

Chapter 22 *The Cabin*

As I have previously stated, our bike excursions seemed to keep taking us further and further away from home. One adventure we planned was to ride our bikes to a local fish hatchery several towns away from Willow Creek. There were many drainage ponds behind the hatchery that took in water from a river that ran alongside the property. These ponds were filled with turtles, snakes and muskrats. Turtle hunting was one of our favorite pastimes and my backyard menagerie of amphibians and reptiles along with other wild animals rivaled the local zoo.

On this day as we arrived at the ponds my friend and I decided we were hungry. There was a corner deli store that made the most incredible sandwiches. For a buck and a half, you could get a freshly baked hard roll with enough sliced cold-cuts to feed three people. My favorite was a straight baloney sandwich with butter and a giant sour garlic barrel pickle. Till this day I still often yearn for that simple sandwich. Anyway, after we got our lunch we decided not to go back to the ponds. Instead we would continue our bike journey and explore new ground. Placing the two brown paper bags in the wire basket that we had fastened to the back wheel on our bikes we were ready to continue. The weather was cool and sunny, a perfect day for bike riding.

I guess we had been peddling for several hours when we crossed over the state line. Neither of us had ever traveled that far from home before, but we were both enjoying the long ride. The road we were on cut through thick wooded plots which eventually turned into rolling hills of corn and alfalfa. The trees once again began to thicken, taking us back into dense woods. This was when we spotted a pond. The river had been channeled through a stone canal to trap enough water to form a small lake. At the end of this pond was an old paddle-driven gristmill. As the water backed up in the pond and attempted its return to the river, it would push a large paddle wheel that turned two grinding stones. By the time of our arrival this mill had long been abandoned but the pond of trapped water remained. Climbing off our bikes we decided to check and see if the old pond was holding any fish. As we circled the back side by the mill, we spotted a small log cabin. It showed no sign of any type of occupancy and seemed to be long abandoned like the old mill. The door was unlocked, and the cabin was thick with dust and cobwebs. We were sure no one had used the place for years. It had two bunk beds although the mattresses were long gone. Only the cords that used to support the padding remained. Each of us stretched out comfortably on the bunks deciding that we were going to make this our secret home away from home.

The two of us went to work cleaning and fixing up the cabin. When we got the chance, we'd sneak into our pantry or 'Fibber McGee' as it was called by my mom. We grabbed cans of peaches, soups and other assorted foods that would be safe from the field mice we shared the cabin with. We spent many a summer day in our home away from home. The millpond did indeed contain bass. With our cabin well stocked with supplies and plenty of fish to catch, we figured that if for some reason it became necessary we could survive in our new-found place just fine. Neither of us knew at the time that our plans would become reality soon.

Chapter 23 *First Rifle*

It was December in the tenth year of my life. My birthday had finally arrived. Two years had passed since the first time I had a chance to fire a rifle at Schneckenberg's hunting camp. My mom was baking my favorite dessert, pecan pie. It would be topped with vanilla ice cream. Lobster was to be the main course of choice on my birthday, sided with scalloped potatoes. All as requested by the birthday boy himself, yours truly.

The excitement that day had been building up inside me till I was about to explode. You see, I had been working on my dad weekly for the past two years to buy me a rifle. Well this was to be the day. I was sitting on the living room couch watching the front door in restless anticipation. If my father came through that door carrying a long box, my dream would finally be coming true.

It was five-thirty when the car pulled into the drive. As he entered the house his path was blocked by a young man who had no intention of letting another minute pass. The box was in his hand and nothing could stop me from locking on as we both entered the house seemingly glued together.

Mom entered the room and insisted that we would have to wait to open presents till after dinner. Suddenly all my favorite foods looked like big hunks of cardboard, just knowing that long box was sitting there. I rushed to finish my birthday dinner, wolfing down a large slice of mom's famous pie with my eyes locked on the long box leaning against the couch.

My parents finally gave in to the suspense. "OK Alan let's open your presents," My mom said with a smile as she placed several boxes in front of me. Ripping off the wrapping paper of the first box exposed a new shirt. The second box contained a new pair of trousers. "Thanks mom, thanks dad!" I blurted as my body started to lift from the dining room chair. "One more Alan," exclaimed my dad handing me another slightly heavier rectangular box. "This is something you're going to need, it goes with the box by the couch." Removing the wrapping revealed a black metal box with the words 'gun cleaning kit' written in gold script on the cover. That's it! Nothing could prevent my flight from the table toward the box by the couch. Pulling off the wrapping paper exposed the words 'Marlin 22 Cal long'. This was it! The moment my two years of begging and pleading had finally paid off. Carefully I lifted the rifle from the box as if it was a piece of fine china. "Easy son make sure you don't point the rifle towards anyone." cautioned my father.

The stock was made of dark walnut. The bolt was polished silver. The barrel was black as night. The rifle had a tubular magazine which ran under the barrel for its entire length. No bullets came with the rifle. It would not be until dad signed me up with the NRA at the rifle range that I would get the chance to use the weapon. At this time bullets were not permitted at the house. Even though I hadn't fired the gun yet, I would still use the cleaning kit every evening, keeping the inside of the barrel spotless. I would also apply linseed oil to the stock until the wood could no longer absorb any more. Strange as it seems for the first week or so, the rifle spent its nights securely tucked under the covers next to me on the bed. Weekends were when I got the chance to fire my rifle. Dad would take me over to the police range every Saturday to shoot. It didn't take long for me to reach the NRA rank of sharp shooter. Competition shooting was fun, but it really wasn't where my interests were pulling me. Hunting was the driving force that linked me to the weapon.

Thanks to Fess Parker's Davy Crockett and Daniel Boone characters, the hunter and mountain man would be permanently locked into my psyche. My love of the wild outdoors had been so deeply ingrained it took precedence over everything I did. This is a love affair that I have had my entire life and it is still haunts me today. Anyway, what I've just told you will bring me to the next part of my story.

Chapter 24 *Gun Trouble*

One Saturday afternoon a friend of mine had come over to the house for a visit. We were hanging out up in my room when he took a small box of twenty-two cartridges from his pocket. The label on the box was stamped CB caps. I had never seen anything like these small cartridges before and they sparked my interest. The shells were about one quarter of the size of a regular bullet, copper in color with an acorn stamped on the rim. I pulled an old shoe box out of my closet and we stuffed it with newspaper to make a target.

These small shells were supposed to be safe for indoor plinking. Sliding open the bolt of my rifle, I pushed one of the rounds into the chamber. Then, taking aim at the shoe box I squeezed the trigger. The report from the charge was almost nil. My Mattel Shootin-Shell Revolver cap gun's muzzle blast was much louder. The bullet hit the cardboard box and stopped dead when it hit the paper inside. We looked at each other with great excitement. Maybe we could get a shot at a rabbit or a squirrel from my bedroom window. No one would ever know we were shooting the rifle. The two of us sat quietly at the window and searched for a target. My neighbors were away on vacation and we were sure we wouldn't be detected.

We could not spot any rabbits or even a squirrel, but we did see some 'chippy' birds as we called them. The birds were flitting around in the hedges between our house and my neighbors'. No longer could we stand to wait for a better target. We took turns trying to shoot these small birds. I do regret doing this for I am against the killing of any animal for any reason other than food for the table. Or, if necessary for the safety of myself or family or farmers crop depredation. Anyway, because hunting was what was driving us at our young age, we put everything including good common sense aside. After we each shot off several rounds without hitting anything, we gave up and put my gun back in its case and left the house on our bikes.

The trouble started when I returned home later that afternoon. As I approached the house I spotted two police squad cars parked out front. The cops were in the side yard and one was pointing his finger up toward my window. My heart stopped. Something had gone terribly wrong and I was sure it had something to do with our shooting the rifle.

Instead of pulling into the drive I began pedaling as fast as I could, blasting right past the house. This was it, suddenly my whole life had changed, and I was on the run joining the ranks of Jesse James and Billy the Kid. "I'm not going to jail, and I'll never let them take me!" I thought to myself. Not quite sure what this meant but understanding that it was the code of all outlaws and now I would have to live by this rule. Tears were flowing from my eyes as my pedaling speed increased. Speeding as fast as possible for the state line, I was heading for my hideout at the old mill cabin. The cabin was well stocked with supplies making it a great hideout until I could figure out my next move. Suddenly my dad pulled up alongside me in his car. Rolling down the window he asked, "Where you heading son"? Choking a bit on my words, I blurted out "I'm not going to let them take me! I'm not 'gonna go to jail!" My dad told me to come and sit in the car for a while. "I'd like to talk to for a bit before you run away." Reluctantly I climbed off my bike and got into the car.

"First of all, son, what you did was very bad. Fortunately for you the neighbors were away. One of your bullets cracked their bathroom window. They noticed it when they returned home this afternoon and had to call the police. You are in a lot of trouble son, but you will not have to go to jail!" The weight suddenly lifted from my shoulders as my dad continued. "You will lose your gun, and it's going to be a very, very long time before you will see another. I'm not sure what your punishment will be at this time, but you will indeed be punished. As far as going to jail, you're very lucky that's not going to happen. Now I'm going to tell you something just between you and me."

"When your Uncle George and I were your age, the two of us sat outside the back of a factory with that old pump rifle you've been looking at down in your uncle's basement. We proceeded to shoot out every single one

of those factory windows. Boy, were we in trouble!"
Somehow this made me feel much better. Even my dad,
who I looked up to with the greatest of respect could
make a mistake.

As it would turn out, it would be six long years
before a discussion about firearms would once again
come up in our household. At that time, I would be old
enough to take a hunter's safety course and actually get
a hunting license. My dad would take me to a local gun
store and buy me a J.C. Higgins, twelve-gauge pump
shotgun. Finally, I would be able to pursue the sport I
longed for. Hunting!

At this point in my story, I would like to leave you all
with some sound advice. If you have young people in
your home and own firearms, please lock them up. Do
not hide the keys in the house. Keep them always on
your person because your children will find them no
matter how well hidden. If you have bullets, do the same
and always remember even if there is no ammo in the
house there is a very good chance young people will
find a way to obtain it. There is a very fine line between

right and wrong with youth. Often these lines get blurred and a young person may choose the wrong way if his desire is strong enough.

Chapter 25 *New School*

There were two schools in Willow Creek when I was growing up, one on each end of town. I'm not sure what grade I was in, but I think it may have been the fifth or sixth, when our class was informed that we were being transferred to the Prospect Street School on the other side of town. Most of us had formed into groups of friends or clicks as they were called, all of us feeling somewhat secure among our peers. Some of these groups were very similar to what some people call gangs. Being forced to enter a new school put all of us face to face with rival groups that considered us to be outsiders or intruders on their turf.

From the first day that we arrived at the new school we had become aware of the fact that we were being watched by various groups from the other side of the tracks. We all felt certain that sooner or later a confrontation would be inevitable. Like ducks out of water we made our way from class to class, hoping not to cross the path of one group. These guys had a reputation of being a very tough bunch. I can still recall trying to fake that I was sick to avoid going to school. I believe many of the other boys from my class shared in these feelings, and no matter how hard we tried it was understood that sooner or later the day would arrive when our group and theirs would come face to face.

During school, although we all felt very uncomfortable there was some protection due to the fact that we were under the watchful eye of the teachers. As we passed in the hall each group shot sizing up glances and secretive comments among themselves. There still was no doubt in my mind that sooner or later the inevitable was going to happen. It was only a matter of time before we would have to meet head on and that was the day we all dreaded. This time of change in our young lives was extremely stressful but as we struggled to fit in, two much larger groups were also having trouble getting along. You see, the United States and Cuba were possibly about to enter a nuclear war. In schools throughout the country air-raid drills were being practiced on a regular basis. Each day we would all have to crawl under our school desks and cover our heads.

The actual concept of a missile strike on us was somehow grossly underestimated at that time. If this feared event was to happen we all would have perished. To our class it was just a way to stop our school work for a time. None of us took these drills seriously or had any real idea of the consequences if an attack actually took place. This was a good thing because we had our own problems to deal with. Eventually the school maintenance crew somehow managed to dig out tunnels in the basement of the school. They strung wire for lighting and filled these areas with folding chairs. Several times a week we would go into the basement for music class. It had become a fun experience which most of us enjoyed. We would sing old folk songs or listen to some famous composer and try to describe what picture the music was painting. This was a pretty good way to get us all used to this environment just in case an actual attack should take place. Looking back now I think that if we were really hit by a nuke the whole building would have probably collapsed. These were indeed strange times. Luckily for everyone this conflict was finally diffused.

Now at this point let me get back to the real problem of the day, recess! During this time of the day we were all sent out to the playground. Although some teachers were present, they were scattered about out of sight of most of us. Several friends of mine and I had gathered on one corner of the field when we suddenly became aware of a second group moving towards us.

This was beginning to look like it was going to be the confrontation we all had feared since the first day we had arrived at this school. So, without looking directly at the approaching group of boys, we all tried to size them up. Watching out from the corner of my eye I could see that one of them stood out. He appeared to be leading the group as they moved into range. There was no question among any of us as to who this was, 'Turl' or 'Turtle-Head' as some called him. He appeared to be twice the size of the rest of the group. I do not believe anyone in their right mind would even

consider crossing his path. I cannot remember what words were used or spoken on the field that day. My fear of what was about to take place took center stage over what was being said. Till this day I don't know why I stepped forward, but there I stood face to
face with this guy that I felt was surely going to kill me.

Strange things happen when people find themselves under extreme stress. There have been reported cases of amazing feats of strength. One man single-handedly lifted a car off someone who had been trapped underneath. The man had no recall of his actions or what he had accomplished. Somewhere in the back of my head I heard the voice of my father, remembering the words he had spoken to me back when he sent me to our neighbor's house for boxing lessons. "Son, if you're ever confronted by a group and you have to fight, always pick the biggest guy. The rest will back off." I'm not sure that this is always the case today, but at the time it was the only thing I had to go by. Suddenly I found myself locked into a wrestling match. I had made my move before any chance of a boxing bout could get started, convinced that if this big guy hit me it would be all over. Quickly stepping forward with my right foot, placing it behind my opponent, I pushed as hard as I could. He fell backwards and hit the ground with a crash. Moving as fast as I could I fell on top of him, trying to prevent him from getting back on his feet. I was in a total panic knowing if I allowed him to get up I would be done for. This was when the strangest thing happened. A broad smile appeared on my opponent's face. No anger could be detected at all, just this friendly smile as he spoke. "It's over," he said grinning. This knocked me totally off balance. I got up and backed away from him as quickly as I could, totally unsure of what was coming next. At that very moment the end of recess bell rang. Both of our groups headed back to the main entrance of the school, keeping a close watch as we entered through the large double doors leading us into the building. There was a teacher waiting for us just inside. "You two, to the office!" First week at school and I was already in trouble, unsure if I should still be mad or not. My opponent's calm state left me totally confused.

As we entered the principal's office we were confronted by a tall, thin man dressed in a light blue suit. "What's going on with you two?" He asked. Silence filled the room for a moment. I was taking the fifth, refusing to say anything. But, as I glanced over at my nemesis once again, I noted that same broad smile I had seen on his face during our scuffle on the playground. "We were just fooling around!" he said to the principal. For some reason this statement had a strange calming effect on me. The words suddenly slipped off my tongue. "Yeah, we were just fooling around". With this, the principal rose from behind his desk looking back and forth at the two of us. "Alright, back to your classes! Don't let me hear any more complaints about you two." We both chimed back "Yes sir!" The walk back to our classrooms was silent. What I was fearing was what was going to happen after school. When the closing bell rang, we all headed for our buses. My eyes glanced all around looking for my enemy, certain he would be waiting for me to reap his revenge. There was no sign of him as I climbed up into the big yellow school bus. Taking a deep breath, I sat in the first seat behind the bus driver. I was safe at least for the day. That was when I noticed several of the other kids that had been with Turtle-Head. They were looking up at my bus, talking back and forth between themselves. No longer could I stand the pressure. I didn't know what they were saying, but it had to have something to do with me. Getting up out of my seat I headed for the bus door and spoke directly to the group that was lingering outside the bus. "One of you guys want to fight? I'll get off this bus and fight you right now!" I still can recall what was said by one of the members of the group. His answer to my challenge was this: "I've got new clothes on, and my mom will get mad if I get them torn or dirty." The group turned away from the bus and the confrontation ended.

That was to be the last time I would have trouble with this group. As time passed, we all would become friends. Some of us played together on the high school football and track teams. We would join in the crazy antics young people get into growing up. When we were old enough, many of us sat on bar stools together raising glasses to our past. So many years have gone by since we were all in school together, life has taken us on many separate journeys. Some have left this earth already, and those we dearly miss. For others, life has taken them far from Willow Creek, but they remain permanently bonded to a special place and time we all shared so long ago. It was only recently I had the pleasure of sitting down with some of my old friends. Although age has changed us in appearance, inside our hearts we remain young. As I sat alongside the big guy some called Turtle-Head, I couldn't help noticing his broad friendly smile that I had seen that day on the playground so long ago.

Chapter 26 *Tunnel Forts*

There was a dead-end court containing around ten homes across the street from our house. If you cut through one of the yards at the back end of the court, you would find yourself in the woods at the edge of a large abandoned hay field. Lying at the bottom of the field was an old dirt wagon road and beyond that were wet lands we called 'the swamp'. This was the place my friends and I could often be found. Turtle hunting or what my mom called 'swamping' was a common practice. There was a laundry room at the back of our house where I was ordered to remove my pants and sneakers before entering. You see, if you are swamping you're usually wading through muck right up to your waist. Often, we collected cattails or punks as we used to call them from the swamp, drying them out on the roof outside my bedroom window until the stems turned brown. Then we would light them. They burned for almost an hour, and the smoke they emitted would do a great job keeping mosquitoes away. Sitting inside the screened-in porch on the side of our house burning cattails was a common practice, until the day things went terribly wrong. Mom had told us it was time to come in for supper. We had been burning several large punks, so we scraped off the glowing tips to extinguish them. Afterwards, we placed them on the shay lounge on the porch and went inside.

It was sometime around three in the morning when my dad was awakened by the smell of something burning. After checking the house and failing to find anything, he went outside and walked around the yard. That was when he noticed the smoldering couch on the porch. As he attempted to drag it outside, it suddenly burst into flames. Lucky for us he did succeed in getting it off the porch. That was the last time we burned cattails inside. But that is not what this story is about, so let's get back to the woods and fields at the end of the court. Fort building was a favorite pastime for young people growing up in Willow Creek. We made several different types of dwellings such as brush pile huts, made by cutting small saplings and placing them against a dead fall. Also, tree forts, and last but not least tunnel forts. It was one Saturday afternoon when a friend and I were crossing the fields heading towards the swamp when we came across two older boys from the neighborhood. They had been digging the most incredible tunnel we had ever seen and invited us to climb down the ladder into the hole and look. We were both eager to go into their tunnel and check it out. When we got to the bottom of the pit they were digging, they quickly yanked the ladder up out of the hole. The two of us suddenly realized we had been tricked, and both of us were now trapped. The two older boys dropped a pail tied to a rope and two shovels. "Dig! If you two ever want to get out of that hole!" The two of us dug their tunnel fort for several hours before they finally dropped the ladder back down allowing us to climb back out. These two boys were much bigger than we were, and neither of us was about to say anything. We both just headed back home. They may have been bigger than us, but I was determined to get even one way or another.

On the side of the driveway by my house was a large White Birch. As a boy, Birches were very prevalent in Willow Creek. Today insects and disease have killed off almost all these beautiful trees. I had built a small tree hut up in this tree. Both my friend and I were sitting high above the ground when we saw Buzz. He was one of the older boys who had held us captive. He was large and considerably heavy. I knew there was no way he would be able to climb up the birch tree. This was our chance for revenge.

We began name calling from the safety of our perch. This totally infuriated Buzz to the point that if he could have found an ax I believe he would have attempted to cut down that tree. Eventually he stomped off in rage and the two of us laughed until our sides hurt. We had gotten our revenge. Several weeks would pass by when I would once again meet up with Buzz who was walking his bulldog Buster. "Hi!" he said in a friendly voice. I was a little surprised, figuring maybe he'd gotten over our tree taunting. Being what I considered a big kid in the neighborhood, I kinda looked up to him. It would be neat if we could turn out to be friends. "Nice dog!' I exclaimed. He smiled and asked if I wanted to pat him. "Sure" I replied. "Just pat him once or twice on the head so he knows you are a friend." With that I reached down and as my hand touched the dog, it exploded. Growling it latched on to my arm. I could barely break free of the animal's grip. I broke into a run for home, my arm had gotten badly chewed. After my mom finished patching me up, she called Buzz's mom on the phone. It seemed that the boxer had a tumor on its head and couldn't stand to be patted. Quickly I realized Buzz had gotten his revenge. This was a hard lesson for me to learn. In life, things will not always go the way you want them to go. Trying to get revenge can often lead to more trouble than it's worth.

Chapter 27 *The Dinosaur*

Oh, just an afterthought about fort building. Some of my friends and I decided to try and build a large tunnel fort like Buzz did. We dug around six feet into the side of the hill at the bottom of the back-hay field. Removing the rocks and dirt from our way as we dug, we suddenly hit something large with our shovels. At first glance we thought it was a root from some old tree in the area, but as we continued to remove more of the dirt from the hole we came to the realization that what we had unearthed was a very large bone.

As we continued to dig at a much slower pace, we started to carefully examine all the solid material as more and more dirt was removed from the pit. Some smaller pieces of bone fragment jutted out of the loose dirt as we were digging. Piece by piece we began removing the bone fragments from the large hole we were digging in that hill. We decided that we would try to put some of the pieces back together at the house of one of my friends who lived close to the fields. His father gave us a large tarp on which we placed all the bone fragments ever so carefully, attempting to try and put together what we had unearthed.

This turned out to be a slow and tedious process. Often, we would make mistakes in our puzzle, not actually knowing what this creature may have looked like. Our crew became excited thinking we had gotten it right only to find out something didn't fit. No longer caring about the tunnel fort, we now had much more important things to deal with. My friend's dad was as excited as we were, and each time we went back to the excavation site he would patiently wait for our return with the next piece of the puzzle.

Our work went on for several days. Sometimes we would dig large, fully intact bones, other times there would be just small pieces. Each time upon returning to my friend's yard, the creature would grow. This discovery appeared to be one big dinosaur. Our group began to speculate on the possibility it may have been a saber tooth tiger, or a mastodon, or maybe some other unknown cave creature. Larger and larger it grew with each day's work at the dig site. We had finally almost completed the puzzle, and our skeleton was returning to its original full glory. So proud and excited we were, standing victoriously, posing by our great archaeological find. My friend's dad came out of the house with a large book containing pictures of skeletal remains Identification. After turning through the pages, he looked back at us with a smile.

"Well boys, looks like what we've got here is the entire full skeleton of one very large bull." Suddenly all our excitement and hard work came crashing down around us. We would never know why back in the 1700's or 1800's when the fields were still pasture, that the farmer would bury an entire steer. Maybe it was typhus or some other scary disease that was prevalent back then. Anyway, we all had spent an exciting week as archaeologists. Till this very day I still find an interest in searching for bones and artifacts from ancient history.

Chapter 28 *Shoveling*

When I was a youngster growing up in Willow Creek, winter snows always seemed to be much heavier than they are today. Of this I can be sure to attest, because as soon as I was old enough it became my job to shovel the white stuff out of our driveway. Once that job was accomplished I would call for my friend next door. We would both take our shovels and head to the next town over from Willow Creek. The reason for leaving our own town was simple, money! You see, some of the towns surrounding Willow Creek were much wealthier communities. Not that there was anything wrong with our town as I have mentioned in the past. It had been built as affordable housing predominately for the increased number of new families when all the men returned home after WW 2. Some of the bordering towns were older established developments that supported more wealthy homes.

Needless to say, that was where we headed to get shoveling jobs. Their bigger homes all had longer driveways which meant more money to clear them. As I was growing up it seemed I was always trying to find ways to make extra money, and a day's shoveling after a big storm could bring you a sizable amount of cash. Things were very different in those days and quite often the folks we were shoveling for would invite us in offering us soup or hot cocoa.

I've lived at my current residence for over thirty years and not once have I heard a knock at the door from kids looking to shovel driveways. Oh well, maybe they are working the wealthy neighborhoods in the next town over like we all did. Somehow though I doubt it, a lot of young people today don't even know what a snow shovel is.

If we weren't out hustling driveway work, we were building snow forts. You see, when the plows clear the roads after a heavy storm they make mountainous piles of snow along the side of the road. This heavy packed snow was perfect for snow tunnels. Thinking back now I realize just how dangerous this was but luckily nothing bad that I can recall ever came from it. If one of our tunnels had collapsed when we were inside, it would have been 'sayonara Charlie' as dad would say.

Anyway, after we tunneled our way through these giant mounds of snow, we dug access holes at the top just big enough to pop up and throw snowballs at cars as they passed by. I'm sure we must have pissed off a lot of drivers as we hid inside those tunnels. Fortunately, we never got caught chucking snowballs as far as I can recall, although the local police made their presence in the area known to us after they had received numerous complaints. Sorry to say, but sometimes when we were growing up we were all real pains in the butt to our local authorities.

The other thing that I recall about the heavy snows of Willow Creek was a special place we called the Villa. No one seemed to know much about this grand old estate. It had stood on its extensive grounds long before the development of Willow Creek. My parents called it a nunnery, whatever that meant. Across the street from the front of this grand old building was a large meadow. In its early days before the town's development, all this surrounding land had been pastures. This piece of land that I'm referring to sprawled uphill toward the town creating the perfect place for tobogganing. It had become a family gathering place during cold winter days.

A warm campfire and hot chocolate could always be found at the top of the hill. By evening young people would gather on the hill to party. The makeup of the field made our flexible fliers almost useless. The runners bogged down in the deep snow and the slay would stop short each time it hit a clump of hay. For this reason, you had to either own or borrow a toboggan. If you didn't, the other option was using a saucer slay or cardboard.

The villa field was a steep fast run. Hidden in the deep snow were logs and boulders that had the ability to stop you in an instant. With each run the snow compacted down more, creating an increasingly faster, longer ride. One night a bunch of my friends and I all gathered at the hill. We had beer and some whiskey, and everyone was getting a little crazy. We were all competing to see who could have the longest run. The hill was packed perfectly for speed. The only light was the warm glow from our campfire. The downhill journey was a blind ride through the darkness.

Three of us climbed into the toboggan and started our descent down the hill. It was an incredible feeling, almost as if we were flying. Realizing we had traveled farther than any of the other slays had all of us totally psyched. What we didn't know was that we had gotten completely off the main path. I'll never know how the telephone pole got into that field but the three of us found it head on. Our toboggan did not survive the crash, but luckily, we all did. The guy in front received the worst of the injury cracking his head against the telephone pole. It was a long wobbly walk back up the hill, but after a few shots of booze and a couple of beers all we cared about was that we had the best run of the night.

Which reminds me of something some friends and I did one day playing in the woods alongside the highway that ran through Willow Creek. We didn't always use our heads growing up. Sometimes emotions just completely took us into overdrive. On this day we were chucking cans. It was fun watching the cars and trucks whack the cans as they passed by. It never appeared to us that any damage was being done, it was just like playing kick the can with cars and trucks. I can't recall how things suddenly slipped out of our hands and the game we were playing had gotten so out of control.

The roadside of the highway was littered with cans and we started chucking them all back into the road. They were all clunking and rattling as they flew about with each passing vehicle. It's strange how easy things can get away from young people. We found ourselves in a total frenzy and completely out of control until we spotted the flashing red light that was making a fast approach toward us. Seeing the cop car shook us both from our madness, it was now time to run. We headed back into the woods and across the fields that took us back into our neighborhood. The squad car was already out in front of my house. We didn't get in any real trouble for our actions that day, but we were warned that next time we would be, if it ever happened again.

Today as I look back on these things, I can't help shaking my head thinking how easy it is for a young person to lose control of his emotions. As many young people often find out too late, their good old common sense had been placed on a back burner.

Chapter 29 *Trap Line*

I believe the year was 1965. Willow Creek was still a very rural place made up of farms, fields, woods and streams. As more and more families began to settle into the area, the towns all started to grow very rapidly. The once vacant land was being swallowed up to make room for new housing developments. Still, there remained enough wooded places for a young boy to fish and hunt or in the case of this story, trap.

As I was growing up in Willow Creek, one of the things my friends and I did to earn extra money was trapping. Muskrats could still be found in the local farm ponds and marshes around the outskirts of the small developing towns. In those days real animal furs were still in demand. Fur buyers would come and pick up the muskrat pelts from us every couple of weeks. The pelts had been skinned, stretched and dried on heavy wire stretchers. Only muskrats that were caught in the fall and winter months could be sold. That was when the pelts were thick and dark in color. We were paid around two bucks a pelt. That didn't seem like much, but it added up quickly and at that time it was enough for us to have spending money.

One of my favorite places to trap was a local fish hatchery that I believe I have spoken about briefly earlier. Behind the greenhouses of the main building were approximately thirty small containment ponds. They were used to grow various water plants and koi, a type of large goldfish. Turtles, frogs and water snakes also made these ponds their home.

During the summer this was a favorite place of mine for catching turtles and snakes for my self-made zoo behind the house. In the cooler months it was the place where we trapped. I believe the owners of the property appreciated that we removed the muskrats from their ponds. The rats dug tunnels from pond to pond allowing fish to escape, often ending up in the river. Also, they would eat the planted aquatic plants growing in the ponds. These tunnels the muskrats dug were the places we would place our traps.

It was late fall and I was setting out my trap lines when I started seeing someone's traps where I had planned to place mine. This guy had many sets, far more than me. Either I would have to give up on trapping the ponds or come up with another Idea. So, letting the darker side of my nature take over, I started checking his runs early in the morning removing the muskrats from his traps and then resetting them. It was my plan that he would think the ponds did not contain any rats causing him to give up on the location and move on.

One morning as I stood knee deep in one of the ponds with one of my competition's muskrats in my hand, I heard a voice coming from behind me.
"How you doing?" said the voice from across the pond on the opposite bank. My heart suddenly wanted to leap from my chest. I'd been caught red handed and had no route of escape. Over on the bank stood this huge guy I was trying to convince to leave. Judging from his appearance he was considerably older than I was.

He was wearing chest waders and had a large backpack. Muscular in build, he stood at least six foot tall. He showed no sign of anger as I climbed out of the pond with the muskrat I had just taken from one of his traps in my hand.

There was nothing I could do but wait to see what this big guy's next move would be. "Been getting a lot of rats from these ponds?" he asked. "Few" I answered back quickly knowing most of the muskrats I'd taken belonged to this newcomer. He was quiet for a moment before he once again started to speak.

"Listen" he said, "I've got an idea! Why don't we become partners? I have a lot of traps and you seem to know where to place them. If we both work together I bet, we will both have a great season." I was totally shocked, still thinking that I was about to get my butt kicked. "OK" I answered back quickly, not having anything else that I could think of to say at this very difficult moment. I guess you could say this was a do or die situation. The two of us spent the rest of that afternoon setting out our traps. A strange thought came into my head as I watched this big guy wade out into one of the ponds with his heavy knapsack filled with traps and equipment.

"Hey!" I asked. "You ever watch the Beverly Hillbillies?" "Yeah" he answered. "Why?" "Well you know the big guy they call Jethro? I'm thinking you look just like him." I guess he liked the show because he looked back at me smiling, the nickname stuck. Some of our trap lines were on the opposite side of the river that ran past the hatchery. He would get me to hop up on his back, then he would carry me across. Never complaining he always carried all our traps and gear. If you happened to meet up with him, you would proceed with extreme caution the way I did that first time we ran into each other on the pond. His large size and powerful build made him look like someone you would not want to ever fool with. The truth of the matter was that he was one of the gentlest guys I've ever met. We never talked about the first day he had come across me pilfering his trap line. We had formed a good partnership that season and that was all we cared about. It was financially the most successful trapping season I would ever have. But as the season eventually ended, I started to think of cementing our plans for the next year's season. This was when Jethro informed me he would not be able to trap with me. When I asked why he told me he was entering the armed forces. As we finished trapping for the year, we shook hands, I wished him luck and we said our goodbyes.

Spring and summer seemed to pass that following year faster than it had ever before. It was now fall, time for me to find places to set out my traps. There was a chill in the air as I pedaled my bike toward the hatchery early one Saturday. Grass around the ponds crunched as I walked out to look for the places muskrats had smoothed down the sweet grass as they moved from pond to pond. Soon they would start tunneling between the ponds, so once the water on the surface froze the muskrats would still be able to forage from pond to pond. I was shocked as I looked across the pond field at the large figure crossing toward me. I instantly recognized my friend's menacing frame as he made his approach. "Could he have changed his mind about the service?" I wondered.

We both finished our greetings. I couldn't wait to find out if he would be able to trap. But sadly, his reply was negative. "I figured I'd stop by the hatchery just in case you were here. We've finished boot camp and now they're shipping us all out. We're going to some place called Indochina. We were all sent home on a furlough for a couple of weeks before we are to be deployed." "What is it like? Do you like being there?" I started shooting questions at my friend. That was when his face suddenly changed its expression. "I hate it! I hate that place!" he grumbled. He then went on to tell me about his drill instructor. It seemed the two of them didn't get along at all. He was always getting into trouble. Two or three times a week his instructor would order some of the men in the squad to take him out berry picking. "Berry picking?" I responded back in a puzzling way. "Yeah, they would take me out behind the barracks and beat me up!" This seemed very strange to me. "What?

beat you up three times a week?" I repeated what he had just told me as if I wasn't sure what he said.

It was hard to believe that anyone would even think of trying to beat up Jethro. It wouldn't be till much later that I would come to realize that the gentle, good nature of his personality was something the drill instructor probably felt he had to remove.

Jethro then proceeded to tell me that at one point he tried to shoot himself in the foot just, so he could get the hell out. He claimed that at the last moment he lost his nerve and moved the rifle barrel to the side just as he pulled the trigger. The bullet just grazed the side of his foot leaving him with a slight scratch. They didn't care, they just patched him up and now they were going to ship him out. I knew little of the place they were sending my friend. There were not many reports on the news at that time about the escalating problems. The military was just supposed to be there as advisers, as I recall. Anyway, as it was I paid little attention to what was on the news in my younger days.

It would be several years before the word 'Vietnam' would become the main topic of conversation at the dinner table between my father and me. Saying goodbye, I wished my friend luck asking him to write and let me know how he was doing. I would not know that this would be the last time I would ever see my friend again.

Considerable time would pass before I received the first of two letters that had been sent from Jethro to me in care of his mom. The wording in his first letter seemed somehow a little strange. It seems he was suddenly having a great time overseas. He told me as soon as I was old enough I should sign up. "You will love this place!" he exclaimed. "We hunt and fish whenever we want. The place is loaded with animals. So, come as soon as you can." This short note seemed somehow out of place coming from someone who was so miserable about being in the service. It would be the second correspondence that would let me know that something had drastically changed for my friend.

He had sent a small package in care of his mom for me. She decided to look at the package's contents. It was pure shock when the box was opened. Placed between two layers of paper were several teeth and a human ear. Immediately she called my mother and informed her that I would not be allowed to have any more communication with her son. This was no longer the gentle giant I had known several years before, setting out our trap lines together. War changes everything.

Another year passed by without any word about my friend, when my mom received a call. She had learned my friend would not be coming home. He had been killed by small arms fire in Vietnam. During the next ten years or so, Willow Creek and all the small towns throughout the USA would see many of its young people become involved in this conflict. They left their families, girlfriends and jobs, giving up all the things young people hold so dear. Forced to travel to a distant land, they would fight for a cause that most would not understand. These are the true heroes of our country.

Some were wounded and would carry the scars the rest of their lives. Others although not injured physically, carried the wounds of war deep inside their heads. All of these young people have sacrificed everything for this country and should be honored and forever treated with the greatest respect.

There are also some like my friend Jethro, who will never come home at all. These young people have given the greatest sacrifice a person can give. They have given their all for their country.

As for myself, I choose to remember my friend Jethro as the gentle giant, the big guy who lugged the large backpack and carried me across the river. Rest in peace my brave friend.

Chapter 30 *Scouting*

At this point in time I would like to thank anyone who has taken it upon themselves to attempt to read the words I've placed on these pages. They have been stored in a dark, musty corner of a small locked closet somewhere deep inside of my head. They do not follow any chronological order and only find their way to paper as I am able to remember them.

My recollection may be somewhat different from actual events since I have no control as to the way my memory has stowed them away. If you find some confusion in trying to follow along, I am sorry. It is my intent to record these thoughts as long as I can. Knowing that at some point in time I will not be able to find anything left in the closet to talk about and this story will end.

Scouting has always played an important part in my life. Teaching me how to get along with my peers. I learned the benefits of teamwork to accomplish tasks too large for one person to handle. How to choose the better parts of my nature instead of making wrong turns which would often lead me into trouble, while strengthening my moral fiber which as a young person growing up was often unstable.

Although my parents did strive very hard to teach me right from wrong, sometimes an outside source would bring somewhat faster results. The knowledge learned about the outdoors I still carry with me till this very day. It's my belief that scouting helped me to deal with many of life's lessons as I grew into adulthood.

The first step in the ranks of scouting was Cub Scouts. Our den, as it was called, was made up of a mix of nationalities. Learning to respect each other's differences, we all learned to work together as a team. We were all friends and spent a great deal of time together even when we were not at our scout meetings.

It was on one of these occasions that three of us decided to take a hike to a sandstone cave I had discovered. The cave was off a road about three quarters of the way up the side of a mountain on the outskirts of a nearby town. We spent the afternoon exploring the cave and its surroundings when suddenly a situation occurred that none of us had expected. One of our friends suddenly felt ill.

He was doubled over in pain and could hardly walk. We knew we had to get him down to the road and find help fast. Thinking the worst, we were sure he was having an appendicitis attack. My other friend and I each took one of his arms and as quickly as we could we brought him down to the road. Then we flagged the first car we saw. The driver turned out to be very eager to help so we packed our friend into the car and headed to the hospital. Several weeks would pass before I would be able to go to visit him at his home. We sat together making plans for the approaching fall trapping season. He had never trapped before and was very eager to learn. I had skinned a muskrat, tanned the hide and attached it to a wooden trophy plank. I brought this over and gave it to my friend as a gift hoping it would help make him feel better. I was somewhat surprised when he told me what had happened to him at the hospital that day we carried him down off the mountain.

He informed me he had somehow gotten a blockage and they had to remove a large part of his intestine. At the time neither of us realized exactly how serious this was. Days would pass and still my friend had not been able to return to school. I visited him often and we both continued to plan our first year of trapping together. I would draw sketches of parts of the river, showing him the places, we would make our trap sets. Both of us could hardly wait for the first frost signaling the beginning of the trapping season.

At school one day a girl I knew approached me and asked if I had seen my friend. She said it was so sad he was dying. This information hit me like a train. "That's not true, I was just talking to him. He is fine, he just needs to get his strength back after his operation. He's trapping with me this year!" She insisted that would never happen.

As soon as I got home from school that day I approached my mom and told her what this dumb girl had told me. My mom was quiet for a while before she started to speak. "He has a type of cancer and he is dying. We wanted you two to continue making plans just for that reason. I'm so sorry."

I can still remember lying in bed that night, tears flowing down from my eyes. "Please God, help my friend get better," I prayed. Until that night I had never asked God for any personal favor, but this was all about to change. That very night as I was praying my dear friend peacefully passed away in his sleep. I believe the Lord did in fact hear my prayer. He took away my friend's pain and gently lifted him up into his arms. "AMEN". Being faced for the first time with the death of a person who is close to you is a devastating experience. Unfortunately, it is one we all will eventually have to deal with. This first loss helped me prepare for the inevitable cycle that I would have to face as I continued my life journey.

Several years passed and I became a nature lodge counselor at a local scout camp. Upon entering the building, I was shocked to see the wooden plaque with my skinned muskrat mounted on the wall. At the bottom of the plaque was a gold plate with the words 'Muskrat

Trapped and Skinned by Alan Sauer.' Just below that were the words 'In memory of my dear friend' who will remain nameless on this page.

Chapter 31 *Explorers*

Scouting was something I was involved in since Cubs. My love of the outdoors and the fundamentals of scouting was a perfect match. By the time I was sixteen I had managed to reach the rank of Eagle Scout with three palms, the highest attainable rank. Sadly, it was also the maximum age for a boy scout at the time, so to continue, the only option was Explorers. It became the decision of my father and several other parents of friends of mine that had also become too old for our troop, to start up the Explorer post. It seemed like a great idea except that we found ourselves extremely short of members. That was when a friend of my dads who was a Sergeant in the local police department came up with an idea. It seemed there were kids in our age group that were finding themselves in minor scrapes with the law. With the help of the police and forceful recommendation from Willow Creek's local court system, these young people were given the option to join our post instead of fines and probation. They had no previous involvement in scouting, but I guess it was better than dealing with the law.

Our membership was growing, and our dads knew that they were going to have to make some dramatic changes in the scouting format for this endeavor to work. These kids' interest at this age were far different from the regular Boy Scout format. The first outing that I can recall was a weekend that we spent at Fort Dix. We went through what you might call a miniature boot camp. Our folks realized that current events put us all in the fast approaching possibility that we might be faced with the draft. We also spent a day on a naval base to learn about this part of the military. Then they set up a co-ed camping trip which went off very well. As I recall several romances took flight on that camping trip including one by yours truly. This was not the boy scout's grandpa remembered. Strange, but as word spread about our Post, more and more kids wanted to join. Explorers had become suddenly a cool thing. The last thing that I remember was the battle of the bands I have previously mentioned that we put on at our high school as a fundraiser. Thinking back, I'm not sure if it was because of my dad's unexpected death, or just the fact that we had all reached an age where the next step in life became reality. For me everything seemed to just stop. I do not know if the Post continued, but I hope it did. Nevertheless, I'm sure it helped at least some of my friends get through some difficult times.

Chapter 32 *The Pits*

There was a place on the far side of town where a few of my friends and I used to mess around at called 'the pits'. A large construction company used it to dig sand and gravel. The land had been completely stripped of all trees and topsoil. All that remained were large open pits of sand partially filled with water.

Looking back now at this playground I've concluded it was by far one of the most dangerous places we could pick to fool around in. The earth around these pits was totally unstable, with quick sand that would suddenly give way under your feet drawing you down into its flooded bottom. We tested this theory several times before we decided that it probably wasn't very smart to get too close to the edge of these pits.

At our age most of us had slingshots. We had found a place in one of the neighboring towns that did wheel bearing repairs. The discarded old bearing assemblies were tossed behind the shop. Using a hammer, we could break open these casings that contained several steal ball bearings. They were the perfect size and weight to be used as ammo.

Originally, we used the old Y-shaped wooden slingshot until a company called Wham-O developed the Wrist Rock-it. This newly designed sling shot was far more powerful and accurate than the old wood versions. I'm sorry to say but during this time these weapons were not only used for target practice. Birds, squirrels, and street lamps were all considered fair game. Anyway, let's get back to the pits.

On this day a friend and I decided for some inconceivable reason, large construction vehicles that were constantly moving in and out of the quarry would make great long-range targets. I guess somewhere in the back of our heads it was sort of like battling the Germans in WW 2, letting the bearing fly and listening for the bang when they hit the target.

We played this game hiding behind one of the large sand piles to prevent the trucks from spotting us. We shelled those German tanks for several hours until one stopped, and two men climbed out looking in our direction. We both knew it was time to run. Looking back now at this memory I can't help shaking my head once again pondering, WHAT THE HELL WERE WE THINKING?

Thanks to some memory jogging from some of my friends, I realized that there was something I forgot to mention about this place. On the property stood an abandoned house. We both decided to go inside and rummage around a bit. This was one of my favorite pastimes since several very old abandoned homes still existed in and around Willow Creek. Although most of these buildings had been gutted long before I was able to enter them, I had learned to check in the rafters and behind walls. Insulation was not always available, or if it was, some could not afford it. In the early days horse hair and paper were often used. These old letters and early publications were very interesting to me for some reason. Also, sometimes treasure was hidden in these places as well.

This house we were rummaging in did have paper stuffed in the walls. I can't remember if anything we found was dated, but the letters were from someone away at sea to his loved one. They were very interesting, and it seemed sad to me that they had been lost to their owner. I wish I could remember if anything was dated but sadly, I cannot. Anyway, I just thought this was worth mentioning.

Oh! One more thing I forgot to tell you about the Pits. It would eventually become the chosen location site for Willow Creeks soon to be built High School.

Chapter 33 *Out the Window*

Next to my bed there was a double-hung window. It was the same one that we used to shoot out of for target practice with my first rifle. The window was just above the porch roof line of our house, situated so it looked out on our side yard.

This was also where I placed the cattails that we gathered from the swamps to dry out, so we could burn them. I always kept a ladder on the roof to get the punks on and off from their drying place. At least that's what I wanted my parents to believe.

Once I was sure everyone in the house had fallen asleep, I opened that window. Climbing out onto the roof I would lower down the ladder next to the fireplace chimney. After slipping on a pair of jeans and a light jacket, down I went. This secret move was only done when a friend or two of mine had also developed a similar method of escape, or if they were spending the night at my house. On this night that I will tell you about, it was the latter that occurred. We were both at the age that our interests were starting to turn toward the opposite sex.

Several blocks up the street from my house lived this extremely attractive girl. Her figure was fully developed and instantly caught our eye. She had a striking resemblance to Annette on the TV show Mickey Mouse Club, who most of the young boys my age had a crush on. Now this girl had a boyfriend that was quite a bit older than we were. He was well known around town to be someone you didn't fool with. I'll never understand how we got the crazy idea to pay her a late-night visit. Maybe it was just the fact that we were out and about when everyone our age was sound asleep. Or I guess it could be blamed on our rising hormone levels, whichever the case we were on a mission. For some reason I cannot recall how we knew which window in the house belonged to this girl, but somehow, we did indeed know.

Picking up small bits of gravel we started throwing them up at her window. Eventually the tapping managed to wake her from her sleep. She turned on her bedroom light and came to the window. She was wearing a negligee and as she opened the window and leaned out our hearts stopped in their tracks.

The two of us were like young bucks that were hanging around a doe while the dominate male was out of the area, desperately hoping somehow for a chance of a meeting. The reality of the situation was that neither of us ever had a chance with this filly. In fact, we would never even get out of the starting gate.

We were very nervous and ready to bolt at the first sign that someone else in the house may have awakened after hearing the disturbance we were making. It's my belief she was totally enjoying all the attention we were giving her that night, reason being each time we started to get nervous and ready to leave she somehow found a way to convince us to stay longer. I don't believe she ever informed her boyfriend about our late-night visit because if she had I'm certain he would have had something much more than words for the two of us.

Funny how I still recall that special night. It gave two young fellas something to dream about rather than thumbing through some girly magazine. In the days to come there was to be no turning back for both of us. We had started on our way to learning a new occupation. It would soon become the relentless pursuit of the fairer sex.

Chapter 34 *Peter and the Goose*

This is a story about two young boys, me and a friend named Peter, and one very angry Canadian goose. So, I will call this Peter and the Goose. Pretty cleaver on my part, don't ya think? Anyway, let us begin.

It was the time of the season in Willow Creek when Canadian geese begin nesting. Now geese lay very large eggs that make a whopper of a fried egg or an omelet. I had somehow learned a special technique to gather these beauties for table fare. It would take a team of two to accomplish this task. So that's where Peter comes into my tale. After telling him how great goose eggs were for breakfast, he couldn't wait to come over and join me in this egg finding adventure. So as soon as he arrived we both headed across the street cutting through one of the yards that skirted the edge of the fields.

As the two of us headed down toward the swamp, I explained to Pete about the technique we would have to use to collect the goose eggs. "It takes the two of us to do this!" I explained. "One of us has to distract the goose, getting it to chase after us so he leaves the nest unattended. That's when the other guy moves in and grabs as many eggs as he can carry, and that is all there is to it!"

Now being that Pete had never pilfered eggs before he was a little nervous about messing with an angry nesting goose. I told him that I would distract the goose and all he would have to do is grab the eggs. It didn't take us long to find one of these nesting birds. The goose had made its nest by gathering a large pile of swamp grass which she had placed by the water on the edge. She would sit on her eggs keeping them warm, protecting them from egg robbing critters such as skunk, raccoon and possum. Not to mention the likes of my friend Pete and I. Slowly I began to make my approach toward the nesting bird. When I had gotten within fifteen yards or so from the bird, it started to hiss. Waving my arms and making verbal noises I confronted the poor creature. Finally, the goose could no longer stand this ongoing assault.

Rising from it nest and extending it long neck straight out forward towards me, it started to move, hissing, with its bill wide open as it started its attack. This was one really mad goose, gaining speed as it started to close in on me. Quickly I started running before the enraged bird could catch up to me. Now it was Pete's turn. He grabbed as many of the large eggs as he could carry and started moving away from the nest. It was looking like our mission was going to be a success.

That was the very moment things were to take a drastic turn, and my well thought out plan was about to go very wrong. Suddenly the enraged goose ceased its attack on me. I'll never know how that bird was able to see my friend Pete as he grabbed the eggs from that nest, I think it must have had eyes in the back of its head. Anyway, the goose suddenly turned and broke into flight in the opposite direction. Keeping low to the ground it flew at my friend hitting Pete directly in the chest. At that point the crazed bird somehow locked its feet in his shirt. Wings flapping wildly, Pete was unable to break free from this enraged bird.

Now I must tell this was the time I should have tried to come to my friend's rescue. Unfortunately, as I looked on at this event something overtook my thoughts. What my eyes were seeing was the funniest sight I have ever witnessed. Pete's arms were flailing about as he tried to free himself from the wild goose. Eggs were flying in all directions as the angered bird flapped its wings violently attempting to maintain its hold. The bird's long neck was thrashing Pete on the face, knocking off his glasses and pecking him on the head like a jackhammer that had gone out of control. All I could do was laugh.

Even as I tell you this story some fifty odd years after the actual attack took place, whenever I see a goose I start to chuckle and think of poor Peter. Thankfully, my friend did not suffer any serious injury. The goose finally gave up on its attack and returned to its nest. It took me the longest time to recover from my laughter. This was Peter's first and last time at attempting the finer art of goose egg pilfering. From that day forward, he would rely solely on the supermarket for his breakfast table fare.

Chapter 35 *Halloween*

Take about a foot-long piece of fishing line. Then tie one end to a nut or bolt. Attach the other end to a thumb tack and what you have just created is a simple device that has the great ability to drive your poor neighbors crazy.

What this story is about is a very special time of the season in Willow Creek. The nights are getting colder, and with each passing day the emerald green woods that skirt the edge of our town begin to go through a sudden colorful transformation. With each new morning sunrise, the tree branches take on a new palette of color and begin to show new warm glows with splashes of red, orange, yellow and brown. Fall has finally arrived in our peaceful town.

In the orchards, the locals can often be seen scurrying about, tugging at heavy laden branches of the now ripe apple trees. Some of them seem to be satisfied gathering the ripe red fruit from the easy low-lying limbs. Others believe that the best apples can only be found on the highest, most difficult to reach branches of the tree. As a young boy I always climbed trees, so I guess you would say I tended to lean toward the latter of these two Ideas.

Rolling pumpkins was another sign of fall. Many of us were carving out pumpkins to make our jack-o-lanterns. We would run through the farmer's pumpkin patch in search of what we considered the perfect one. My requirements were simple. It would have to be large, but not so big that I would not be able to lift it. Solid orange in color without any white or flat spots. These blemishes occurred when the pumpkin was left lying on one side for too long without being turned. Finding the right one required rolling each pumpkin over to check for possible imperfections.

My mom would help me prepare the pumpkin by taking a knife and cutting a circle around the top stem. Once this was accomplished it was my job to scoop out the remaining pulp and seeds. The pulp would be used for pumpkin pie. We then washed the remaining seeds, covered them in cooking oil and salt placing them on a baking sheet to roast in the oven. I would always have a small bag of them in my pocket during this special time of the year. We would then draw a scary face on the pumpkin which we cut out the best we could. Placing a candle in it finished the job. We put our jack-o-lantern outside by the front door as a seasonal decoration. These ongoing events signaled the approach of one of my favorite days of the year, Halloween!

All the young folks in Willow Creek were waiting with eager anticipation of this special day, trying to decide what kind of scary costume we would choose for trick or treating. In the early days of my childhood we had no TV. We had to rely on radio to hear scary stories about monsters, vampires and ghosts. Eventually my folks brought home our first black and white television. Scary movies such as Dracula and Frankenstein were popular shows we watched in preparation for our much-anticipated special day.

When it finally arrived my friends and I would all gather together dressed in our Halloween costumes. I can recall the large pillow case mom gave me to carry all the candy that I would collect from our neighbors. It is interesting when I think of how we all ran around at night unchaperoned, ringing strangers' doorbells, trick or treating as it was called. Even when the rumor started to spread around town that there was the possibility that someone was tampering with the candy, our parents
simply said that they had to go through our bags to check the candy before we ate anything.

It's been some sixty years since I was a boy growing up in Willow Creek. It's curious that many of us walked or rode bikes to school without any fear of being accosted by gangs or sexual predators, drug dealers or the like. Sad but I believe our society may be traveling downhill in the wrong direction. We did have some simple campaigns on child safety. Don't talk to strangers, don't accept candy from strangers (except on Halloween) as I have previously mentioned. Still we were all able to travel around town on our own without fear.

As we all grew a little older, my friends and I became aware of something that went on the night before Halloween. Cabbage, Goosey or Mischief Night was what we called it. On this special eve the night before Halloween, it was customary for the older kids to go out after dark and run around the neighborhood causing mischief. Most of these antics were harmless fun like throwing a roll of toilet paper up into the trees in someone's front yard or ringing doorbells and then running off. Kind of strange that kids would run around town bothering folks and then the next day return to the same houses and expect candy. Only in America!

This was to be the first year that my friends and I would be allowed out on Cabbage Night. There were several of us on this adventure. We all dressed in dark clothes, so we wouldn't be spotted by anyone. I can't recall how we had all become educated as to the ways of mischief making. It must have been passed down from an older generation, but I have no recollection of it ever taking place. Anyway, as the three of us gathered together it seemed we all had secretly grabbed at least one or two items from the house that could be used in our mission of mischief.

The knocker was the first thing we put together. The first requirement was that the house we were going to place this knocker on had to have a house across the street from it that had a hedge of some kind that we all could hide in. We used the tack and nut tied on each end of a foot-long string that I spoke of at the beginning of this story. Then we'd sneak up to the side of this person's house and press in the tack just below a window. One of us pulled a spool of fishing line from their pocket which we attached to the bolt. Then we unwound the line as we crossed the street and hid behind the bush.

Now there are several things you need to remember when executing this prank. If you see a car's headlights approaching you must quickly let the line, go slack preventing the car from catching the line. The same procedure must be repeated when the victim of the prank comes outside to see what is knocking. Hopefully he will not catch the line with his foot, and as soon as he goes back inside the tapping procedure is repeated. If the homeowner figures out what's going on, it's time to head through the backyard as fast as you can.

The three of us played this prank until we started to get bored. Moving on we ran up and pressed a few doorbells then ran away. But we also quickly became tired of doing that. We needed new ideas to satisfy our lust for mischief. We started passing ideas back and forth between us. Someone suggested we get a paper bag and fill it with dog poop placing it at someone's front door and lighting it with a match. When the owner came out and tried to stamp out the fire his foot would be covered in poop. We all thought it was a great idea, but we had no paper bag or a match. Furthermore, we couldn't figure out how to find enough dog poop to fill the bag. Also, no one wanted to be the one in charge of picking it up. So, we decided to scrap that stinky idea.

One of us had a can of shaving cream and we all agreed that it was a good choice. We had each grabbed a bar of soap before we left home. This was it, we decided, we were going to soap car windows. The trouble was we were running out of time. We all had to be home by 9 o'clock as I recall. Many of our neighbors had put their cars in the garage for the night and we were getting desperate. That's when suddenly a strange thought came to all of us at once. One of our dads' cars was outside of the garage and we decided that this was it. We were going to soap, and shave cream our first car no matter what. I think each of us must have used an entire bar of soap on that poor car, not to mention the shaving cream.

Still we all headed for home satisfied we had been very successful on our first cabbage night adventure. This was 'sort of a rite of passage for me. I felt I was finally able to do something like the older kids. I slept well that night knowing that the next day I would still be able to collect enough candy to last me a month.

The following morning my dad woke me early with a message. "Your friend's dad called and said you guys did a great job of soaping. He said he couldn't wait to see what the car will actually look like after you guys finish the job." It took us a good part of the morning to clean off the car. Somehow this just wasn't quite what we had planned. Thank goodness no one had wax!

There were problems that came with Cabbage Night. It's a thin line between harmless mischief and flat out vandalism. Some young people from Willow Creek and the other close surrounding towns started to become destructive to the neighborhood property. It eventually got to the point that the police departments felt it was time to issue a curfew.

By the time this curfew had been implemented most of my friends and I were passed the age of trick or treating. In fact, most of us had started to drive and we no longer found ringing doorbells and soaping car windows amusing. Still most of us felt the electricity that the fall season brings to a young man's spirit. Not wanting any problem with the police, someone in our group came up with a plan.

We asked the local police for permission to stay out past the curfew if we assured them we would not bother anyone in the neighborhoods. I guess the cops decided it was one bunch they didn't have to worry about and they said OK. Packing everyone in four or five of our parents' cars, the egg wars were about to begin.

Each of those cars in our group was considered the enemy. We all started cruising around town until we spotted one of the other cars in the group. In those days cruising was a common practice for us at the age of seventeen, looking for girls and meeting up with friends at the local pizza parlor. This night was different. Each car had armed themselves with cartons of eggs. The plan was to try and ambush one of the other cars and pelt them with the eggs and then escape. After several small skirmishes, we decided we would need to purchase more ammunition before we would be able stand up to a major assault by more than one of 'the enemy' cars.

It seems the local merchants had another plan. Toilet paper, paints, shaving cream, soap and eggs would not be sold young people. This meant that to get our ammo we would have to drive to other towns which also had curfews in place. They knew nothing about our arrangement with the Willow Creek police department. I believe it was a convenience store in a neighboring town that finally sold us our supply of eggs. Almost immediately after leaving the store we saw the flashing red light of a squad car.

When we explained to the police officer what we were up to, he told us he knew nothing about any arrangement that was made with our town, and if we were caught out after nine we would be apprehended. We slipped back into our hometown loaded with eggs and began to cruise around looking for the enemy. We had several skirmishes but were not able to inflict much damage. A better plan of attack was needed.

The traffic light was to be where the major battle would take place. Three cars had been following our car when we hit the light. Stuck at the red light we knew this would not be good. Our car was getting pelted from behind and sustaining serious egg damage. Then suddenly the tables turned as the traffic light changed to green. I started to drive slowly as our team back lobbed eggs at the cars stuck behind us. I can still close my eyes and see one of our friend's windshield so covered with egg he could no longer see, scraping to clear a spot so he could drive.

The war finally was over, now all we had to do was explain to our parents what the hell we did to their cars. This would be the last time most of my friends and I would celebrate Cabbage Night and Halloween, but I will always remember that crazy time.

Chapter 36 *Spaceman*

I think it was my freshman year at Willow Creek. Some of my friends and I were walking home from a school dance when this lady called to us from one of the houses on the street. "Boys," she said to us. "Would you please look at this? I have to show someone". She pointed up at a large star that seemed to be hovering, moving up and down and from side to side. She told us that it had appeared every night for the last week or so, and she just had to tell someone about it. I thought it was cool, so I asked if I could use her phone to call my mom, so I could show her. Upon my mom's arrival at the scene and seeing what we were looking at, she borrowed the woman's phone and called the police.

When several police cars arrived, we were informed that they were aware of the object and that there was a second one which the officer pointed out to us. He then told us to enjoy what we saw, but as far as anyone was concerned they did not exist. He said that the report had been filed and that was the end of it. My mom made phone calls and inquired with the weather and air traffic control and was informed there were no weather balloons or planes in the area. One of the police officers stated that what we were watching did not exist. I guess sometimes things just can't be explained.

Before I go any further, so you don't think I'm totally nuts, you must understand that these are actual events. They occurred, and I leave it to you to decide whether to believe them or not. So here we go with the continuation of this story. (Jerry's little man).

Jerry was a friend of mine who lived on the next street over from me. He had an early morning paper route on the weekends. One morning he was dropping off the papers just before daybreak, when he came upon a small man in a silver suit with a blacked-out face. The man was holding a box with lights on it and appeared to be pointing it at a bush. Jerry was startled and said nervously to the man "Who are you?" At this point the man turned the equipment which looked something like a camera at Jerry. That was enough for the poor kid, who at that point broke into a run and never looked back until he was home. From that day on he would not do his paper route. Frequently Jerry would stay at our house for dinner but refused to walk the few blocks home after dark. My mom would have to drive him in the car. Both mom and I teased him constantly about the sighting of the little man, but he didn't care. He knew what he saw and that was that. Hope I am not boring anyone with this, but the story does get better.

A month or so had passed since Jerry's meeting with ET. Mom had finally backed off teasing him because Jerry seemed to get very edgy whenever the subject of spacemen was mentioned. This is where my story takes another turn. It was around 9 pm one evening, and my dog Joe was pacing at the door to go out. My mom got his leash and took him out for a walk. As they went up the street Joe started to growl and hair on the back of his neck stood up. He became completely unmanageable. This is when mom saw the silver, snow suited, little man with the blanked-out face coming down the opposite side of the street. He was pushing something that resembled a wheel barrel.

As the little man got directly across from my mom, she spoke to him. "Isn't it a little late for you to be out little man?" It turned to face her for a moment, then continued down the street to the corner and vanished. Mom never teased Jerry again. She never liked to talk about what she saw that night either. We had to press her to tell anyone the story. Was it just a little boy walking in the early hours of the morning and late after dark in a silver snowsuit and black mask on his face in the middle of summer? In my final post on this subject I am going to fast forward some twenty years to an incident that I believe will tie this whole story together, so stay with me! As I had just said, many years had passed since the Willow Creek sightings. I had moved up to the northern part of our state and purchased a 1970, four door Fleetwood from a judge friend of mine. The reason I bring up this car is because it will help me to tie everything together with the rest of this story.

One Saturday morning I heard a knock at the front door, standing there was one of my neighbors. He was a big guy, probably six feet six or so, weighing close to three hundred pounds. "Alan, I'd like to ask you a favor. A friend of mine is thinking of a run for office in the county. He is very large like me, and we were wondering if you would consider driving us on the weekends to make some political contacts in your Fleet wood?"

The man I was asked to drive had become famous during the riots in Newark. I agreed, and each weekend off we would go. At the end of every day a state trooper and the man I was chauffeuring along with my neighbor would return to my house where we would play cards, drink beer, and talk about my new friend's past which I found incredible. It was at one of these poker sessions that the subject of UFOs came up. I began telling the men the same story I've told you. This was when my neighbor suddenly became very quiet. He had a very serious look on his face as he started to speak. He wanted to show us something, but it was classified material. He said if it ever got out he would deny that the conversation ever took place.

After we all agreed, he carefully removed an old

picture from his wallet. The photo was of my neighbor and another young soldier, both in their early twenties in military uniform. The two were standing at attention, holding the wrists of a very small man-like creature that was hanging limply between them. The little man's feet hung down, just about touching the ground. He was wearing what looked to be some type of shiny outfit. His head was covered by some type of mask which blanked out his entire face. My neighbor started to explain how when he was in the service he had been stationed in New Mexico. He and the other soldier in the photo had been ordered to witness the autopsy of this little man who had been killed when his craft crashed.

He did not know the reason they ordered the two of them to witness this, but they followed their orders. I was shocked at first as a million questions raced through my head, then I laughed at the thought of mom and Jerry's little man. My neighbor told me the body was like us but in a much smaller size.

The craft he had flown was a small round ball made of a metallic material that was resistant to drilling or cutting. I asked him how it flew, and he told me they had no idea. He did say he believed the suit and a utility belt the creature wore were copied for use by our government. The equipment design was later used by NASA. In the years that followed, leaks about this subject claimed that a contract was given to a large company, possibly GE or Westinghouse to study the craft. This explained why there was a sudden burst in new technology that did not exist prior to the discovery of the crash, such as microchips, and some other technological advancements. These things can only be considered as speculation. Unlike the photo that I saw which I felt was one-hundred percent authentic.

I hope some of you found interest in this story. Sorry if it was to long-winded. I tried to keep things as short as possible. At this point I will end this story with a simple note, "That as for me and grandpa, WE BELIEVE!"

Chapter 37 R*ight, Wrong and Somewhere In-between*

If you walk back behind the Villa Marie Claire, cross the field and walk over the old cement bridge, you will come to a canal. Turn right and follow it to the end and you will have arrived at the place where this story begins.

The old mill was built back in the 1700's. Part of a large estate that was comprised of a hotel / tavern, way station with stable slave quarters and a grist mill. As a young boy this was one of my favorite places to fish, play and get into mischief. The latter is what I will tell you about in this story.

One day as a friend of mine and I were snooping around the mill we suddenly became aware that the upstairs part of the mill had been boarded up and locked. We started wondering what we might find inside. We noticed a tree that had grown up past a window on the second floor. Both of us were experts at tree climbing so it was easy to shimmy up to the window.

As we peered through that clouded, dirty old window we couldn't believe what we saw. There in this dingy, dust filled room of cobwebs, mice and squirrels nests was a virtual museum of ancient historical treasures. Horse drawn carriages and early publications from the founding days of this great country. Stoneware, quill feather writing implements, old player piano rolls, slave ankle and neck chains, and the list of treasures went on and on.

They were all randomly strewn about creating nesting places for the rodents that had made the place their home. It didn't take much time for us to get that old window open. Once accomplished, we decided we needed to find something to pack this new-found treasure in to bring it home. Returning to the house I grabbed my dad's old army duffel bag. This would do just fine for our purpose. We returned to the mill and started combing through the piles of strewn debris. The first thing I found was a stack of 'The Books of Common Sense' written by Thomas Paine, 1775-1776, and Montgomery Ward catalogs from the late 1800's. The list of publications is too many to mention. We filled the duffel bag with as much of our find that would fit. Then tying a rope to the bag, we lowered it out the window. I couldn't wait to show mom our treasure. That's when something that we hadn't even thought about occurred.

After showing off all that we had found, I suddenly became aware of a worried look on mom's face. "Where did you two find this stuff?" she asked. That's when we both suddenly realized our mistake. "It was in the old mill!" I answered already knowing what was coming. "Alan this doesn't belong to you." "But mom nobody cares about this stuff, it's just getting eaten by rats and stuff." I knew this wouldn't work but I figured it might be worth a try. Somehow my mom had gotten the phone number for the caretaker and after apologizing she told us to take what we had stolen back. The caretaker met with us by the old stable. I'm unable at this time to tell you what or how we both were punished for this crime, but I now we both were in big trouble. Just fessing up to the caretaker seemed to be bad enough.

Several weeks would pass by when my mom

received a call. The man at the stable told her he understood that she was trying to teach us both right from wrong, but he wanted to inform her that the owners of the estate had removed all the contents from the mill, placed it in a pile and burned it.

He was saddened that she had us return our treasure. He asked my mom to have us stop by the old stable, he had something he wanted to give us. We did as he had asked although we were somewhat scared thinking we were going to be in more trouble than we had been in already. At first, he seemed a bit cross with me, but after a while he mentioned about the great loss of all the artifacts that had been destroyed. That's when he handed me a small bundle of papers. "Here, I thought you might like these!"

There were several of the original liquor licenses from the estate boarding house. Also, some very interesting quill-pen written shopping lists for goods from Drew Hardware in Paterson NJ. Not the priceless antiques that we had taken from the mill, but I appreciated them just the same. As I started feeling a bit more comfortable, I asked if he had ever heard of the rumor about hidden treasure somewhere in the old slave house. It seemed I had heard this same tale in every old house that I had the chance to look through, but I still figured it was worth asking. He smiled, "I doubt that very much due to the folks that lived there. If in fact there is it won't be for long! They plan to knock the building down next month." I was unable to help myself: "Do you think it would be OK if I looked one time?" He was quiet for a moment then he smiled, "Go ahead, just be careful." I rushed home and grabbed a few tools that I thought we might need and called my friend. Together we searched that old house from basement to attic to no avail. The walls were packed with horse hair but nothing else. We also found the eves in the attic in the same condition as the walls. It looked like the caretaker was correct in his thinking.

But just as we were about to leave I noticed something strange about the floorboards in the entrance room of the house. What I spotted was a small, foot-long piece of flooring almost dead center in the room.

This cut board made no sense to me. The condition of the surface showed little sign of wear as if it had been covered by some type of mat. We quickly went to work prying up that short piece of floor. As the piece popped out it exposed a red cloth bandanna. Could this actually be the rumored treasure? Reaching my arm down into the hole I grabbed hold of the cloth bundle. My hands shook as I unwrapped the tightly tied kerchief. The cloth contained several coins which I was unable to identify, and paper money in small denominations from the bank of New York and Connecticut. Not much of a treasure to us but this small amount could have meant a great deal to a slave.

I couldn't help wondering why whoever this money belonged to never came back to claim it. Anyway, my mom eventually donated our treasure to a museum for safe keeping and that's all I have to say about that old mill.

Chapter 38 *Booze Runners*

It was early in our freshman year at high school when a friend of mine informed me that he had obtained a large supply of booze. Try as hard as I could I was unable to get him to tell me how it had been obtained, only that we had more than the two of us could ever consume. Our first mission was to figure out where to hide our stash, so after giving it a great deal of thought we both agreed that the old train station in town would be the perfect place.

On the side of the building was a small crawl space, that by removing a board or two we would be able slide the stuff under and then replace the boards. We both agreed no one would ever have a reason to look in such a hiding place. Our next move was to celebrate our newly acquired find.

A bottle of Four Roses seemed like a good choice. Slipping the bottle in one of our coats we headed up to White's Pond. Neither of us had much experience with hard liquor and it took no time at all for the two of us to down the bottle. That's when the fun started. First, we both staggered around on the banks of the pond laughing as we stumbled about. Not long after that we both started to feel ill. We spent a good part of the afternoon attempting to purge the wretched whiskey from our systems.

No way could we return home in such a condition. Although I pried as much as possible, my friend still refused to tell me how he had managed to possess all this alcohol. Just the same, I kept an eye on the local papers for any report, but nothing ever appeared.

Today I believe that I'm able to have a good guess, but this will remain my secret in this story. Anyway, after our initial exposure to whiskey it seemed that we both lost the taste for it. That's when we decided our best bet was to see if we could sell it to our upperclassmen. The beer, vodka and gin we decided to keep for ourselves. Our method to move the other stuff was simple. We would wait for a school dance or a pep rally then let the word out to some of the older guys at school. For a while we both had good income from these dealings, but as time went by we all started to drive and with the help of fake ID's the booze market eventually collapsed. Thinking back, I can't help but wonder if when they refurbished that old station they found any of the old stash we left behind.

Chapter 39 *First Car*

On my sixteenth birthday I talked my dad into letting me get my first car. A 1949 Flathead Ford. The car had a 'do it yourself' paint job. Midnight blue with white pinstripe, and a pair of dice hanging from the rear-view mirror. It had a cool look of a hot-rod but looks were all it had. I can still recall the day we drove over to the next town to take a look-see.

The car had been advertised in the local paper for a hundred bucks. I can't even remember if it ran at all. Somehow, we were able to get the car to its new home in the backyard. My plan was to fix it up so that when I turned seventeen it would be ready for me.

Now my friends and I knew nothing about cars. Still we started taking things apart and then hopefully putting them back together. Dad kept a back seat on this project, watching us as we tinkered with that old car. At one point I can recall taking out the trans for some reason. The job was accomplished by removing the front seat and unbolting the transmission from the floor of the car.

For several months we tinkered with that old car before finally losing interest. An odd thing about those old flat head motors was that if they were not turned over regularly they locked up tighter than a drum. One day as I returned home from a friend's house, I found dad and a neighbor pushing the old ford up and down the street trying to get it started. Once they got the car running my dad parked it in front of the house for several days until someone came and towed it away. By that time, I didn't mind saying goodbye. It just wasn't any fun having a car you couldn't drive.

I guess that old Ford somehow satisfied my lust for a car for a year or so. But as I approached the age of seventeen dad started to hunt for what he considered the safest car he could find. It turned out to be a gray 1954 dodge. This car was built like a Sherman tank. Mom gave it the name 'Honorable Grandfather'.

The car had a clutch which you had to use to get into first gear and reverse. After that it became an automatic trans. I really loved that old gray tank. It indeed helped me stay safe during that first year of driving, teaching me what happens when roads get slick and the driver fails to slow down. The car took me across several lawns, removing small trees and bushes as we went without receiving as much as a scratch to its old faded gray paint job.

Together we traveled down many back-dirt roads and drove far out into the old farm fields. It seemed I was hoping for the opportunity to get closer to a girl I had become fond of. We made many trips over the state line together to a small delicatessen that would sell us quarts of beer or an occasional bottle of an orange flavored liquor call Tango. At the time Tang was the drink of choice for our astronauts, so the spiked version had to be good for us. Anyway, nothing lasts forever and eventually I started thinking about getting a newer car. As it turned out a friend of mine had gotten a job at a Dodge car dealership. He had ordered a special newly designed 1968, 440 magnum Dodge Charger. To my knowledge it was one of the first of its kind in the state.

He had ordered it special and had it blue printed and balanced. This was the car of a young man's dreams.

I'm not sure why, but after only a few days my friend's dad decided the car had to go. My guess was he thought it spelled trouble in the hands of a young driver. So that was when I made my move. The car was rather expensive as cars go in those days, having a sticker price of around four thousand and five hundred bucks.

As I was growing up I never realized it but being and adopted child I've come to the current conclusion that I was somewhat spoiled. I'll never know how I was able to convince my dad to let me get that car, but it did indeed happen.

It was painted a dark midnight blue metallic paint with a double bumble bee stripe on its tail. The car's rumble as it cruised down the street was loud enough to be heard a full block away as it made its approach.

Willow Creek was entering the time of the muscle cars. Chargers had a three speed, Torque Flite auto trans. I added cheater slicks which had two tread grooves which made them street legal. The car ran stock except for the 456 rear. Dodge had designed an incredible rear pumpkin. I was able to pull off on the side of the road, remove a few bolts and pull the stock rear and pop in the track pumpkin in a matter of minutes. The only fuel the car liked was Sunoco 260. Pricey fuel at somewhere around a dollar something per gallon as I recall. The car was only getting five and a half miles to the gallon, so we were always looking for gas money. We would cruise around until we found someone who wanted to race. We would pull up alongside another car we wanted to race, revving our engine. If he gave us a nod, we would show ten fingers. If the second nod came, we were on. Ten bucks was not a lot, but it was all we could afford to put up for a race. If we won, we could head across the state line looking for girls and beer. This was the thing we had been waiting for all week (Friday and Saturday nights).

Whenever I pulled up at a store or at a bar, people would crowd around the Charger peering in the windows, most looking on in envy. On one occasion as I drove across the town of Willow Creek a police officer pulled me over. Beginning to panic, I nervously handed him my license. I already had gotten some points for speeding and didn't want any more.

Although I was pretty sure I hadn't done anything wrong, the cop walked around the car and informed me that the police were going to get a few of these cars. What he really wanted was to drive my car. A sigh of relief suddenly came to me as I got out and quickly handed him the keys. He took the car for a quick spin around the block, handed me back my keys, said thanks and took off. That's the kind of car the Charger was. By 1970 every car manufacturer had jumped on the gas guzzler, big block bandwagon. Outlandish paint jobs, bigger engines and louder exhausts. Each one trying to capture a piece of the action.

There was a wide array of bolt-on parts that would help boost these cars performance, as if any of them really needed that. Almost every weekend we all would cruise the local highways looking for someone who wanted to race.

The method I used when racing was called power braking. I would snap the shifter into first gear and holding my foot down hard on the brake, apply my other foot to the gas, bringing the RPM's up to 5000. I'd let go of the brakes and floor the gas when the traffic light turned green. If we were not at a light, my passenger would count off on his fingers.

Dodge suspension was incredible, tracking the car straight as an arrow when it came out of the hole. If I was running the 456 rear, the car was usually wound out in the first eighth of a mile. Although it was supposed to be a quarter mile race, once we pulled away two or three car lengths we would shut down and considered the race won. I'm sure if we ran out the full quarter mile a few more of those races would have been lost, but I wasn't about to let on to that.

A few of the lighter body cars we raced were very 'squirrely', as I used to call them. Mainly because of over revving the engine and the lack of weight in the tail end when coming out of the hole. For this reason, I always gave them a wide berth at the line. One of the worst of these cars was the Z28 Camaro. I'm only mentioning this now because I will have more to say about this car before the end of this story. There were several guys that would race with me more often. It was a way for them to see if the bolt-on improvements that they had done on their car helped. One guy worked for a Ford dealer. He drove a Mustang Shelby Cobra GT. Each time we raced, and the Charger would win, he would take his car back to the dealer and they would bolt on more stuff.

Hi rise manifold, open headers, bigger carburetor, etc., etc. With each new add-on I noticed his 'souped' up car was getting closer each time we raced. The last time I would race him his car would finally beat me by a nose. But not before they had installed a Detroit Locker in the car. This made the Mustang practically useless for driving on the street.

This locked rear prevented the car from taking a turn at speeds higher than twenty-five or thirty miles per hour without the car hopping all over the place. "Well guys, Congratulation's! You finally managed to get a fully modified production car to beat my stock Charger!"

All good things eventually come to an end, but I still can recall the last time I would personally drive the Charger in a street race. I did not know the guys I was racing or even what kind of car they were driving. All that I remember is that we had pulled up to a traffic light on the local highway several towns away from Willow Creek. The light was green as we approached so we were forced to stall traffic until it went red, so we could begin our countdown. It was unfortunate for me but somewhere in the backup of cars there was a cop. When he figured out what we were up to he radioed ahead. One mile or so up the highway they set a roadblock. As I climbed over the hill the cops came into view. I began looking desperately for a place to pull off that damn road, and not being able to find any kind of exit I knew what was coming. I was busted! Now at the time of my court appearance I was carrying points on my license, this was going to put me over the top. They were going to pull my driving privilege for sure. The judge asked the cop how fast the car was going. Smiling the cop responded that he had no idea, all he was able to see was the blue streak fly away at the light. It was my hope that maybe I had a shot if he hadn't caught my speed.

That's when the judge chimed in. "One thing I can't stand is when a driver goes slow and then fast and slow at a light. I'm going to find you guilty of obstructing traffic." I was dead. These points put me over the top and they were going to pull my driver's license. After that I allowed my soon to be brother-in-law to be the wheel-man when we went cruising.

The last race that I'm able to recall that we had with the car before I was finally forced to put it up for sale was against a 427 Corvette. We had been cruising the highway a good part of the night and had not found any races. That was when we noticed the 'Vette sitting on a trailer on the side of the highway. Now the Charger had smoked a good number of 427 Corvettes, and it always felt good beating one of these icon's.

We asked the guy if he wanted to race. He seemed

not to be interested at first. But after raising the wager fee he finally agreed. We were positive this was going to be easy money. Then a bad thing happened as the guy turned the key and started his engine, rolling the car down off the trailer. This was no street 'Vette. We were about to race a full-fledged funny car.

I did the countdown as this monster car started its rev-up cycle tacking somewhere around eight-grand. The car was so loud we couldn't hear our own words. On ten, the car exploded and cleaned ten car lengths before our car broke from the hole. Well, we paid the guy off and headed for home feeling like we had been really dumb allowing ourselves to be taken so easily. But it was cool to see that funny car run. Placing the for-sale sign on the Charger was a sad day, but I somehow knew it was time to say goodbye. There was something else that came to Willow Creek along with the fast cars. It was far darker and more sinister.

One night I had been sitting at the local pizza parlor when two of my friends pulled up. They said they had just installed a new four-eighty-eight rear in their car and wanted to know if I would like to come with them for a test drive.

Now this was the Z28 Camaro I had spoken about earlier. I thanked them and said I was going to pass. It was kind of late, I was tired and was going to head home. That would be the last time I would ever see them. The rear they had installed malfunctioned. It locked up causing them to lose control hitting a large tree. Both perished.

By the time I would leave high school some fifteen of the young people from Willow Creek and the surrounding towns would lose their lives. All would be directly related to street racing, high speed and something I will speak of in the next chapter, alcohol!

I was glad I was able to safely walk away from this dangerous game. Terribly sad for all those who didn't. They would all be sadly missed.

Chapter 40 *Photostats*

The town of Willow Creek was in a state where the legal drinking age was twenty-one. So, unless you knew someone who would turn their back, most of the bars and clubs were off limits.

For most of my friends and I, our best shot was to cross over the state line to where the legal age to purchase alcohol was eighteen. As soon as one of us turned seventeen and could drive we started to head upstate. Word spread fast and we learned which places were the easiest ones to get served in. Sometimes it was just a matter of who was at the counter. If the lady was working that night you would get served but if it was her husband, he would card you.

Carding was something common in our younger days. The draft had been activated due to the troubles in Vietnam. Once we turned eighteen we received a draft card from the government. This card was what most bars and clubs used for identification to check our age when we entered the establishment.

Well it didn't take us long to figure out that by taking someone's card and taping off the name and address, we could then make a photostatic copy and insert our own.

Some of my friends started using these fake cards at the age of fifteen. Usually if you got into a bar a few times and they got to know you they stopped carding and you were considered a regular. I must admit that I was spending way too much time in these places. On several occasions the owners insisted that I go to the kitchen and eat something before drinking any more booze. Strange now that as I recall we had very few troubles with drunk driving, considering we ran back and forth over the state line every weekend and we were always over what today is considered the legal limit.

Back then the government would from time to time run ABC checks in the bars. These guys would come in and check to make sure no one was under age. Most of the bars that we hung out in were somehow notified when this was to happen. We were either sent to the kitchen or told at the door not to come in. I never ran into one of these guys but I'm positive that they were around.

During my senior year we had gym last period of the day. During the warmer months they would make us run on the track. I would park my car on the street below the football field. As we rounded the turn on the track I quickly rolled down the hill to my car, climbed in and headed for the bar. Funny that no one ever realized I was missing.

Chapter 41 *About Me*

As I was growing up in Willow Creek our schools required us to take certain tests. Now I will tell you these things really make me nervous. If I knew all the answers beforehand I believe my results would still be the same: 'FAIL'. My sister has told me that my mom said I was LD in school.

Being adopted I had to assume one of my paternal parents must have passed on this strange trait. It wasn't something that ever really bothered me much except when I had to read a homework assignment. You see if I didn't use a ruler on each line I was all over the page. Numbers were also a problem for me. They just fly around in my head 'sort of like a bird that was caught in a hurricane. I was often in trouble for not doing my homework. My reading and math problems often caused me to cut up in class. As I got older cutting classes had become a common event. That was the only way I was able to cover up for my deficiency. I just couldn't keep numbers in my head and spelling was totally impossible. So, I was always failing Math and

English.

Until one year when I had an English teacher who taught creative writing. Suddenly my grades went from failing to A's and B's. Telling a story was something I always loved to do. In school we had these tests we were forced to take. They were designed to find out what a person should be when they grew up. Every one of these SAT test I took throughout my entire time in school pointed to the same two directions. Forestry or police services was number one and a writer came second.

Well I loved the outdoors, so it was easy to understand why forestry kept showing up in my results. Although I never followed these leads for a career, my life has always been deeply immersed in this subject. As far as a writer, well that's another story. I always figured that was a dumb glitch in the testing results. How the hell could I ever become a writer when I can't spell worth a bean. Having these shortcomings never really gave me much of a problem in life because I found that when a person has a weakness in one thing his body compensates by making them strong somewhere else. I was always very good at fixing stuff. Working with my hands was what I did best. If something didn't work right and I was able to see and touch it, I probably could fix it.

The other strange trait I have is that my life emulates one of a grasshopper. You see I've lived my life like a kid in a candy store, often becoming over obsessive about something in a field that allows me to become expressive. The trouble with these obsessions is that just when I'm starting to get pretty good, I quit and hop to something new. Thus, the 'Grasshopper Effect'. Thanks to modern technology I'm now able to try one of the things that those old SATs always suggested. Spell check is helping me immensely, except when it suggests a word that takes me totally off the course of what I'm trying to say, and I am unable to tell the difference. So, if you are reading any of this stuff and suddenly find something strange in the words I have written, I apologize for my shortcomings.

Chapter 42 Friday Afternoon

It was just after our lunchtime as I recall, when several of my friends and I were coming back into school. I usually brown bagged lunch and we were permitted to eat outside on the lawn. Upon entering school, we were all directed to go into the cafeteria instead of our homeroom. This was strange I thought, as we walked into the large room of folding tables and chairs. Everyone in the entire school had gathered in the school cafeteria. We all started to question what was going on, but no one had an answer. Whatever the reason, we'd all rather be there than in class.

We were sitting for what seemed like a long time and most of us were starting to get restless. I made a paper airplane and chucked it at one of the other tables. Their table fired back with popcorn left over from someone's lunchbox. A food fight was about to escalate when we heard the buzzing sound of the school intercom. "May we have everyone's attention please!". The message was repeated several times until the cafeteria finally calmed down and the large group became somewhat quiet.

I don't recollect the exact words that came over the intercom that day, but they hit everyone in that room like a train. What we were told was that our president, John F. Kennedy had been assassinated. Most of us had little interest in politics back then, but the popularity of the Kennedys' was an altogether different story. They were both looked at almost like a prince and princess out of a fairy tale. He was the prince charming of every young girl's dreams. His pretty young wife had become the fashion setter for an entire country.

From her hair style to wardrobe her look was what every young girl tried to emulate. It was no surprise that this young magical couple took center stage in every newspaper, and TV news program.

As young people we all loved them, so when that message came over our intercom it hit that room hard. The entire cafeteria suddenly went into total shock. Everyone started crying or were just too stunned to say a single word. Even I started to well up with tears in my eyes. I guess you could say it was giant group gathering of emotion.

For weeks there would be nothing on the TV but footage of the Dallas assassination or the Kennedy funeral. Strange when I think back now, even the weather was miserable. It seemed like it rained constantly for several weeks as the country mourned for their great loss. It's my opinion that such an up-welling of emotion over one individual or couple as they were, will never again be seen. The emotional reaction that shook this country over those several weeks during this horrible event would make it a horrific one of a kind moment in history.

Chapter 43 Who Is in The Closet?

Often as a young boy I would find myself not being able to sleep. It's odd how simple things can easily affect your ability to get a good night's rest. Often, it was in anticipation of an event that was soon to take place. Christmas, birthday, or the opening day of fishing season. This list goes on and on. Another common cause of disrupted sleep was when a young person partook of too much of a good thing.

My folks often accused me of having a hollow leg. I would overeat if mom cooked one of my favorite meals, topped it off with some homemade apple or pecan pie covered with a large scoop of vanilla ice cream. All these disruptions of sleep can be completely understandable and I'm quite sure anyone reading this will be familiar with this strange phenomenon.

Fear was another thing that could directly attribute to lack of sleep. If when growing up you were ever bullied by someone, you will understand how this can have the nasty ability to disrupt sleep for days on end. Worrying about your grades on a report card or the results of an upcoming test also can be the culprit of a restless night. Another sleep disrupter for me was the fear of loss, dreaming that something happened to my mom, dad, sis or even one of my pets. These are just a few of the reasons a young person might find them-selves sitting up in bed in the late hours.

Putting all these things aside for now, what I wish to tell you about is something of a much darker nature. As a young boy there was another reason for my loss of sleep. It always manifested itself in the quiet, wee hours of the night. Simply forgetting to close my bedroom closet door was all that was needed for this strange sleep disruption to begin.

Our house was heated by forced air ducts. When the furnace fired, the air would be pumped through ducting and be delivered into our rooms. As this occurred there would be just enough airflow to cause the closet door to move slightly creating a creaking sound that was just loud enough to prevent me from sleeping.

As I looked around the bedroom trying to figure out what and where the strange noise had originated from, I saw them. They made not a sound as they slowly crept out of the partially opened closet door, appearing to look more like shadowy figures as they quietly moved about the room. Several of these intruders wore strange cone shaped pointed hats. Their clothes consisted of a shirt which frilled at the waist band and tight, stocking-like pants. Shoes that pointed at the toe much like the top of their hats. Not a sound could be heard from these tiny gnomes as they moved along the baseboards of my bedroom wall.

Some of them were dancing on top of the heat vents, while others climbed up on the window sill across the room on the opposite side from my bed. Although I was well covered with blankets, they were still able to see me in the dimly lit room. The ones on the window sill were the first to spot me hiding under the blanket. Each one of them pointing their fingers at me.

"Mom, dad, mom, MOM!" I called out loudly waking my parents. My mother rose up out of her bed and entered my room turning on the light. What's wrong Alan? Quickly I glanced about the room. "Nothing," I said to myself. "Mom, I heard something in the closet!" She walked over and shut the door tight. "Go back to sleep Alan, it was just your imagination, everything is OK." She kissed me on the forehead and left the room.

Well, I'm telling all of you now, I know what I saw that night. It wouldn't be the last time those gnomes would pay me a late-night visit after I forgot to close the darn closet door. Thankfully as I grew older their visits became less and less until they finally ceased to come at all.

Many years have passed since those days of elvish visits. On one occasion years later, as I sat drinking a few beers with my son, now a grown man, the topic of nightmares came into our conversation.

"Dad, the one thing that really bothered me when I was growing up was my closet door! If someone forgot to close it, these gnomes would come into my room in the middle of the night." I couldn't help laughing, now knowing I wasn't the only young man who was plagued by these elvish midnight visits. Then I started thinking, back when I was a boy I knew nothing about these what I will call 'garden variety gnomes'. You know! The type people put out for decoration on their lawns and in their gardens. It's my belief that they originated somewhere in Holland, or possibly Germany. Could it be these early Europeans were also visited by strange little creatures, when they were young? Perhaps, that's why they started making duplicate statues of what they saw, placing them on the lawn around their homes.

I can't help but wonder who else can attest to these late-night visitors. So, if after reading this story, you have also been visited, please drop me a line. I'm just wondering how many other folks from Willow Creek have had the pleasure of one of their late-night visits?

Chapter 44 *The Find*

Although my bike had become my major form of transportation, sometimes walking was the only way to get to certain destinations. There are so many places to be discovered were no road exists. Most of us tend to only follow the paths that are paved with blacktop, causing us to miss everything that lies in between. The older we become the less interest we have in finding out what's just over the next hill. We all tend to close our eyes to everything around us, and only concentrate on places where the highway can take us. When I think back now, I can still remember the times my friends and I decided to leave our bikes at home and chose to explore the places the road would never see.

We crossed the Saddle River by an old cement bridge. This took us to a canal that was built long ago to divert water from the river to drive the paddle wheel, which turned two huge grinding stones at the long-abandoned grist mill. These old buildings dated back to the times of the revolutionary war. As a young boy I would spend a lot of time exploring this place but, on this day, we were heading up over the top of mountain in search of new adventure.

Crossing the top of the ridge, the woods suddenly began to thin. We were now standing in a development of giant mansions. We continued following the quiet street that ran past these homes till we came to a cull-d-sack posted with the sign dead-end. At the bottom of this court the woods continued once more. I will tell you now that the place we were in that day was several towns away, but by traveling as the crow flies we were able to get to this area much sooner than if we had taken our bikes.

We walked in the woods for around a mile or so before we came to the edge of a farm. Along the wood line was a large garbage pile. Crates of fruit and vegetables that had spoiled and then were discarded. Old rusted farm equipment that had long lost its use, and all sorts of other junk that had been dumped there.

We often rummaged through places like this because you just never can tell what kind of cool stuff people will throw out. As we climbed about the pile, suddenly we spotted what looked like a large bear lying in the rubbish. Both of us instantly froze in fear. It took some time for us to realize that this animal was showing no sign of movement whatsoever.

Slowly with a great deal of caution we proceeded to move closer. Could it be that the farmer had shot the animal and left it on the garbage heap? But as we got close enough it was clear that it was not a bear, or at least not one that had been recently living. It was a large rolled up bear skin rug. How cool! A find of a lifetime, I thought to myself. This was going to look so neat lying on the floor by my bed. Finding this bear skin rug was neat, but what was rolled up inside was going to prove to be far more interesting. Each of us grabbed hold of an end of the large, rolled up fur, moving it away from the rubbish pile to a flat open area in the field where we could take a better look. As we started to unroll the rug it became obvious there was something inside. Neither of us could believe our eyes as its secret content came into view.

Carefully rolled up inside were thirty-two cartons of assorted brands of cigarettes. Ten dollars in one-dollar bills, and a pocket full of change. What in the world had we found?

Now up until this point my friend and I would sometimes sneak a butt or two from our folks, head out into the back fields and secretly puff a bit. Well that was all about to change since we had found the mother lode. Quickly grabbing the two ends of the rug, we moved our treasure back deeper into the woods just in case anyone came back to claim it. Both of us agreed we should go back to the garbage heap and take a second look just in case there was something else that we might have missed.

As we came back into the field by the dump there was a station wagon parked in front. Standing next to the car was this tall slim figure of a man. Not sure what to do, should we start to run or see what he wants? Something both of us noticed at the same time was the fact that this guy was wearing a gun on his hip. "What you boys doing around here?" he asked. Both of us were ready to bolt, but for some reason we didn't. Possibly because the only people that we ever saw wearing a gun were police.

"We're from Willow Creek"! We exclaimed. We just hiked across the river and came up here through the woods. He seemed to be nice and easy to talk to, telling us he was the caretaker for the property. So, after we told him our names, he introduced himself.

"You can call me Stony!" Strange name, I thought to myself, sort of like a cowboy. Anyway, after a bit of small talk he pulled a small pouch from his pocket. He then poured some of its contents into a small piece of paper. "You boys smoke?" he asked. Both of us nodded yes, not saying a word about the cartons we had just hid. He smiled and proceeded to roll two more cigarettes. We spent that whole afternoon hanging out with him. He showed us the location of a secret Indian sandstone cave that sat up on the ridge looking out over what now was a town. We told him we really liked the gun he was wearing.

Pointing over at an old beer can, he instructed me

to pick it up and throw it as high as I could. Before the can hit the ground, Stony had drawn his pistol from its holster and hit the can six times. Never even to this day have I seen anyone who could shoot like this man. He took a rifle from the back of the station wagon and we all took turns shooting cans. Stony had instantly become our new best friend. Rolling several more smokes and handing them out to us, he boasted how he had started to smoke when he was just around our age. For some reason neither of us spoke a word about the bear skin or its contents. It was starting to get late in the afternoon and we both decided we had better head for home. After saying our goodbyes and setting up plans to meet up with Stony again, we headed on our way. We hid our cigarette cartons inside several plastic bags beneath a bridge not far from our house, then took the fur rug back to my home placing it on the floor next to my bed.

Several times we would return to that farm dump, but never again would we run into our friend, Stony. It was like he just vanished. I believe he may have known more about those cigarette cartons than he let on, although I didn't think much about it at the time. I'm quite sure someone must have committed a robbery, stashing the stolen goods back behind the garbage dump where we had found them.

Was he just a cool guy, or did Stony have another motive for friending us and sharing his smoke? I'll never know for sure. We took all the unfiltered cigarette packs which neither of us cared for, and we shoved firecrackers in them. Lucky and Camel were just too strong for our liking. I was thirteen and my friend was two years older. He was into acting cool and looking like a tough guy, so we each took a pack of smokes and headed to one of the nearby towns, our hair slicked back into a DA (Ducks Ass) with Alberto VO5. Although my hair wasn't very long I did my best. To look cool, we always carried a smoke behind our right ear, and the rest rolled up in the sleeve of our T- shirts. By the time we smoked the last pack of those cigs, both of us had become totally addicted to tobacco.

Chapter 45 *First Encounter*

I guess I was around sixteen or seventeen when we first met. My sister had invited several friends over to the house. Now I had never met this one girl before and I'm not altogether sure how well my sister actually new her either. I'm thinking this girl was interested in being introduced to me and had arranged a visit with my sister in order to do so.

She was an attractive girl, with long dirty blond hair and a very nice figure as I recall. She wore a pair of red, skin-tight jeans and a pull-over sweater that fit her form to a T. Up until this time I had several girlfriends, but the relationships were fairly innocent ones. Although I was totally unaware, something was about to change. So, after some informal introductions someone suggested taking a walk in the back fields by the house. I was not intending to go with them, but my sister's friends coaxed me to come along. We crossed the upper field and headed down toward a string of dense saplings that skirted the edge of the old logging road leading to the swamp. I'm not altogether sure how the next events took place. The girl with the red pants suddenly sat down on the grass. She told my sister that she was just going to rest for a bit, and to go on ahead. "I'll catch up in a couple of minutes," she insisted.

I told my sister and her friends to go ahead. "I'll stay with her till she's rested and ready to continue. We'll catch up in a bit." I was beginning to think to myself that this whole thing was a pain in the butt. Why did I ever get involved with my sister and her dumb friends. Anyway, I stood there waiting for this girl to get up. Not really having anything in common for us to talk about, we basically just stared at each other. I noticed this strange smile or grin on her face like she was up to something. This was making me even more edgy. What the hell does this dumb girl want? I had finally had enough of this nonsense and extended her my hand to help her get to her feet. She reached for my hand but instead of rising she gave a sudden yank and pulled me down on top of her. What the? She was still wearing that strange grin when she asked if I wanted to kiss her.

I didn't know what to say, "I don't even know your name" I told her. Still smiling, she introduced herself.

At this point I will stop my description of this encounter for I have no intent of revealing any of the intimacy that came from this or any other romances that I have had the pleasure of sharing. I only have mentioned this because it leads me to what I want to talk about in this story. What I would call my first 'Love'. You see, I believe most of the young men and women in Willow Creek and in all the other small towns throughout the country, sooner or later meet someone who turns their life upside down for the first time. Whether it is due to their first romantic interlude, or just the first time they feel that this may be the only person they wish to be with in life. The side effects are often the feeling of walking on air, loss of appetite, not being able to sleep, and putting all the things you normally love on a back burner. These symptoms are all warning signs that you have become love struck. This condition can often be a parent's worst nightmare. The fear that if the relationship goes too far, it could begin to threaten the dreams and expectations they have for their child. It's common for parents to force a breakup any way possible in order to defuse this fast track relationship. As for the young couple, they are blind to everything around them.

All common sense gets thrown to the side of the road. I can still remember how our family had taken a vacation to a camp somewhere in Maine. This should have been something I would have loved to do, but because I was being forced to leave the girl behind, threw me into a state of total depression. I spent the first entire week lying on my bunk bed. Finally, after a week of gloom I picked up my fishing pole and headed down to the lake. Something happened during those two weeks we were away. The first thing I did when we returned home was to pick up the phone and call the love of my life. There was something strange in the tone of her mother's voice when she answered the phone. She informed me that -----was not home. I continued trying to make contact, but sadly all my calls went unanswered.

After several weeks I was finally informed that my girlfriend had met someone new while we were away on vacation, and she would not be seeing me anymore. I will never know if this was orchestrated by her parents or just her decision, but whichever it was made little difference to me. The romance was over.

This loss to my young life created a new condition. You see as I walked down the same street that my feet floated on only several weeks earlier, they now hardly left the blacktop. Every girl that passed seemed to look like my lost love. I would never be able to recover from this great loss, or so I thought. My life was over.

A month had passed by when friends of mine convinced me to attend a dance in a nearby town. That's when I saw her. She lived two towns over from Willow Creek. Her long blond hair stopped just short of her waist. I knew instantly she was the only one for me. The new true love of my life! For sure?

Chapter 46 *When You Can't Lose*

One Saturday afternoon as I was taking a shortcut through the back fields heading home from a friend's house. I happened to come upon his older brother, who was holding a large steal ball in his hand, resting it against his shoulder. My curiosity got the best of me, so I sat quietly and watched to see what he was up to. Tucking a large metal ball tight under his chin, he started bending down toward the ground then back up in a sort of bobbing motion. Suddenly his one leg kicked back out like that mule that used to chase me when I was fishing.

He exploded with a forward thrust letting go of the steel shot he was holding. It flew through the air as if it was shot from a cannon. "Wow!" I said, observing how far that shotput actually traveled. Next, he picked up a flat saucer shaped plate that in track is known as a discus. He wound his long legs up like a spring in a back and forth method, then spinning his entire body round and round in a sweeping motion, released the platter. It looked like some kind of UFO as it flew through the air. I became fascinated watching him practice. As the days went by, he also built a high jump and a pole vault setup in that back field. I watched him as he continued to work at his craft.

After observing my friend's older brother, I made the decision to give track a try. When the high school track season started I 'kinda felt like I knew a secret about him. You see, no one in Willow Creek or any other town around the area for that matter, had ever come across anyone like my friend's older brother. He was a one man track team all on his own.

My track and field ability was nothing great, but it did manage keep me in good shape for football. I was always eager for my events to be over, so I would be able to watch my friend's brother sweep the field. Pole vault, broad jump, hurdles. Shot put, discus and almost all running events found him unstoppable. I've often wondered if he had received a college scholarship or performed in the Olympics. Anyway, I just felt he deserved mention in these Willow Creek memoirs.

Chapter 47 *Football*

In my freshman year at our new high school I decided to join the football team. I had been playing football with a sandlot team sponsored by the dad of one of my friend's. The team was called the Red Devils. It was a great way for us to learn about teamwork. One of my friends was way too small for this sport. Some of the bigger guys found a way that he could become a great addition to our team. Goal line stance! He was small and light enough for the linebackers to pick him up and throw him up over the goal line.

We had used our secret weapon several times and my friend had become a football star. Back in my day anyone could be successful. It was what a person puts forth, regardless of his size. If you make up your mind to succeed, you can be victorious. So, by the time we started high school we were already well indoctrinated into football.

High school football always started in the summer before classes began. Most of us were out of shape that first year and practicing in the heat of summer was a real killer. I can recall a friend who was also on the team spending the night at my house. I think his family was away on vacation, so my folks took the two of us back and forth from practice. Every single bone in our bodies ached. We were both so sore we couldn't even sleep. It seemed like we had just finished practicing and it was already time to start all over again.

I believe we both would have liked to say the 'hell with this', but each day we found ourselves back on the field. By the time school actually started, we were in better condition than we had ever been before. For some strange reason, the coaches had chosen me to be one of the co-captains of our team. I wasn't crazy about this idea, but I did the best I could to keep my teammates spirit up and our drive at its peak. As freshmen we all tried our best and we had a pretty good first season, but we were totally overshadowed by our senior team.

There was nothing that could hold a candle to our high school varsity. They were some of the biggest, toughest guys you'd ever want to meet. I'm not sure, but I believe that varsity team made Allstate that year. Anyway, being the captain of the freshman team, I decided to throw a party at my house for the entire football team. My folks were eager to meet every member. Anyone who knew Mr. and Mrs. Sauer knew the door was always open to them. Never had our house been so full of people as the night of that party. Although I'm sure that the varsity players may have had better things to do that night, they still came to our party. That made me, and my folks feel really good. Funny but I can still recall the music that was being played that night over and over again. The song Rip Van Winkle was on the record player. The crazy beginning was the sound of an elf shouting: "Wow-wee, ha-ha-ha-ho, a strike!" Over and over again. Some of the older guys would go in and out of the house from time to time. I wasn't sure if they were having a nip or two or smoking a butt. This didn't bother me because at least they all stayed. It was no accident that two of the biggest varsity team members were hanging around in our kitchen. I believe they were staying close to the food cause these two guys were as big as a house. They were rough-housing a bit when the kitchen door flew off its hinges. Gosh, I thought, my dad will flip out. But instead he just laughed and shook his head commenting, "Boy, they're big boys!" That's just the way my parents were.

Chapter 48 *Greatest Loss*

When I was almost nineteen years old I was attending a school for airplane mechanics during the day and working nights in a small pharmaceutical packing plant in Willow Creek. I was still living at home at this time, preparing myself to soon move into my own apartment. Mom stayed at home taking care of the house as did most of the married women in Willow Creek.

My father had worked for years at a printing company. He was a type setter and print editor. The place he worked was about to be bought out by another company. Dad couldn't risk being laid off, so he took a job in the city. As things turned out, the company kept all the original employees and dad had made the move for nothing. I don't believe he liked the new job very much. Although he never complained, he was hitting the bar car on the train fairly heavily. Often by the time he arrived at the house you could tell he'd had one too many martinis. Sometimes he would start to fall asleep at the dining room table when we were having supper.

We all felt bad for him, but we knew he had done what he felt to be totally necessary.

It was one late afternoon on a Friday as I recall, mom was in the kitchen preparing dinner when she happened to look at the clock on the wall over the sink. "That's strange!" Already five o'clock and Hank's still not home from work! Must have been some kind of trouble with the trains." Then she went back to work cutting up some vegetables for the meal she was making. By six o'clock there was still no sign of my dad. I was due to be at work at the plant, so I finished off a quick plate and headed for the door. "Mom call me at work when you hear from dad!" She said "OK," nervously pacing back and forth in the kitchen.

Just past nine o'clock, I heard some kind of commotion at the back door of the plant. Leaving my work station, I walked to the back to see what was up. Standing there with the night foreman was a Willow Creek police officer who was a friend of my dad's, along with the minister from our church. My legs suddenly started to buckle right under me. Not a single word was spoken as the two men each grabbed one of my arms. There was no need for them to say anything, I knew what this visit meant.

The next morning my dad's cop friend picked mom and I up and drove us into the city. We entered this old brick building and took an elevator up to the fifth floor. The three of us entered this room which was totally empty except for a wooden, four-foot-high railing fence that formed the shape of a square in the center of the room. My mom stayed with the police officer as I walked out into the room approaching the edge of the railing. When I glanced down I realized that there was an opening in the floor. You could clearly see down to the fourth floor below. Looking down I saw my dad lying on a large concrete slab. He had a few small cuts on his head and that was all I noticed. So, turning back to my mom and dad's friend I nodded my head yes. Mom instantly broke down so as quickly as we could we moved her out into the hall.

All my dad's personal belongings had been stolen. Fortunately, dad's police friend went back to the city the next day and was able to recover his personal things. It seemed the ambulance driver rolled my dad before bringing him to the morgue. Pressure was placed on the driver and he returned dad's stuff. The police officer told my mom not to tell me what actually happened to my father. A year would pass before I would find out that he had been murdered for a paycheck. If I had known about it from the start, I would have loaded one of my guns and stalked the robbers, killing them on the courtroom steps without ever thinking twice about what the ramifications would be. Thankfully, that never became reality. Strangely, even in death my father was still looking after me. My dad gave his all fighting for his country, caring for his family, running an explorer post for kids, many of which were having troubles in their lives. To suddenly take a man like this from the world for a few dollars is just too much for me or any decent person to deal with. We buried my dad in a Veterans Cemetery. Years went by before mom also passed. At her funeral, a woman I didn't know, approached and told me mom wanted me to place her ashes on my dad's grave. Although she had remarried, I understood. I did what she had asked.

My  Dad

Chapter 49 *Table Fare*

If you've ever stood alongside a meadow marsh, the kind found along the outskirts of Willow Creek in late summer, you would know there was something magical and almost dream-like about the place. If you listen carefully, you will hear the call of the red winged blackbirds as they fly from cattail to cattail searching for insects and the small seeds inside these now ripened plants. These beautiful black birds with large patches of red crimson and gold on their wings hang precariously from the cattails as they bob to and fro in the breeze. Multi-colored dragon flies buzz about hunting for mosquitoes and other small flying insects that live among the tall swamp grasses. Bullfrogs disturb the silence with their loud clunking call as they try to convince a mate to join them. The far-off sound of the cicada also breaks the quiet solitude of the meadow with their shrill pitched song. Gentle breezes whisper hisses as they try to find their way across the grassy fields.

Summer was the time for spending a lazy day on White's Pond fishing for bass or catfish. Cats always liked to feed after a summer rain or at night. A red bobber and a can of worms was all a boy needed to catch enough fish to make a fine supper. You could also hunt for turtles, snakes, and frogs on any one of the many small farm ponds that could be found around Willow Creek.

Now there is something I'm about to tell you some may find upsetting, but in my youth was accepted as normal procedure. The catfish is a slimy fish with no scales. It is endowed with three bone stingers. One on each side of its head, and also one on top. If you manage to let this fish stick you, the sting is very similar to that of being stung by a bee, only a much bigger wound. Great care had to be taken when handling this fish. The technique I had learned to use was simple. In order to grab the fish, you opened your hand grabbing from the belly, letting one of the side stingers fit between your first two fingers, and carefully closing your hand so that your thumb is just under the spike on the fish's other side. The top stinger is now pointing away from you. If this is done properly you will not get stung. Once you've caught a bucket load of fish, it's time to get them ready to cook for supper. This is when things may seem upsetting for some, so if you're squeamish don't look at this part.

Taking a hammer and some nails we would bring our catch over to my catfish tree. Each fish would get nailed through the head into the tree. Then an incision would be cut around the fish's throat, grabbing the skin with pliers at the place you've made the cut. Then pulling straight down, you have just gutted and skinned the fish which is now ready for the frying pan. You can dredge the fish in batter mix or just use straight butter, salt, pepper, and some sliced onion. You've made a wonderful catfish dinner! Frogs were also skinned but only the legs were fried. Two techniques were used to procure the frogs. The first way was a stunning stick. Once a frog had been located you would sneak up as close as possible. Then you would attempt to smack the frog on its head, stunning it so you would be able to pick it up and place it in your sack. Sometimes instead of using a smacking stick I would use my fishing pole, taking a small piece of swamp grass and placing it on a hook. If you shook this around in front of the frog, he would try to eat it. Bingo! You've just caught dinner. Now I can understand how some of you that are reading Willow Creek might be disturbed by some of the things I've written. But it is important to understand that certain beliefs and concepts have gone through many changes from the 1950's. Back when I was a boy, fishing was something you did for food. Not all people fished, but if you did it would be considered unjustified cruelty to catch fish for sport. There was no such thing as catch and release in my early boyhood. Neighborhood fish fries were commonplace, and my mom was an expert at making fish chowders. We would all catch and clean the fish we caught and save some for the community fish fry.

I can recall one fishing trip when we had caught a large stringer of fish. It was a mix of sunfish, perch and bass. I was so proud of our catch that I couldn't wait to show my mom. Lifting up the full stringer I shouted, "look mom!" not realizing dad had unfastened the stringer from the boat. Needless to say, as I dropped the stringer back down into the lake, our entire catch of fish swam away. See! Sometimes I did practice catch and release. Several days would pass before my dad would forgive me. For the last thirty years I've had the great privilege of helping to manage five lakes in my community. We have introduced four new species of fish to our water system, and replenished stockings of fish that we felt were diminishing for some reason or another. I am on the water almost every day and release 95% of the fish I catch. I do still keep some for supper sometimes.

Chapter 50 *Turtles and Snakes*

Turtle and snake hunting were also one of my favorite pastimes back when I was young. By late summer, our side porch and yard were transformed into a zoo.

Amphibians and reptiles of all shapes and sizes could be found in this backyard habitat. Possum, squirrel, rabbit and raccoon or any other orphaned animal that I would find ended up under my care. By late fall most of these creatures were released back into the wild. Now in case anyone might be wondering how to collect snakes and turtles, just listen carefully and I will teach you some tricks. I do require that you all be sworn into secrecy.

What is required of a young boy when turtle or snake hunting is a very keen eye. Turtle or Snake eye is the name used to refer to anyone who has managed to master the high level of expertise that is required to be great in this field. So, let me give you my secret techniques although I'm sure other hunters will tell you they have developed their own secret methods.

In my opinion, my technique is the best that has ever been developed. "First!" Find a swamp or farm pond. Some of my favorite places were two local fish hatcheries. One of which I have previously mentioned in one of my stories about trapping.

These places contained numerous ponds full of green slime and weeds, which are the best places to find all kinds of snakes and turtles. Now some of my competitors choose to use a fish net when catching turtles. The big problem with this is the heavy amount of slime and aquatic plant life found in the ponds. Nets tend to get totally bogged down in the muck and the turtle gets its chance to escape. Snakes slide out from the webbing in the net, making this method totally useless. So, let's get started!

First, let's check out the necessary equipment. You will need an old pair of jeans and sneakers, because you are about to find yourself up to your waist in muck.

If snakes are what you are hunting one stout stick is advised. Also, you will need several burlap sacks.

As quietly as you are able, approach the water's edge. At this point let your eyes begin to carefully scan the surface. What you're actually looking for is something protruding above the green algae slim. This would be the critter you came for! A snake or turtle.

Large ones are pretty easy to spot, but it takes a real pro to spot a baby turtle or snake. Once you've located you prey begin to wade into the swamp. If the head suddenly slips out of sight don't panic. This is where a novice usually makes his biggest mistake, believing the critter has spotted him and has already made his escape. The fact of the matter is ninety percent of the time he has not moved at all, still sitting just below the surface of the muck right where you had spotted his head. So never take your eye off that spot where he was last seen. When you reach that particular place where you saw his head, open your hand, and spreading your fingers slightly apart, begin to gently plunge your arm down into the muck. If it was a turtle you spotted, you will feel his shell, then simply grab hold and you've got him. At this point I would like to give you a warning. If the head you spotted was a large one, it was probably a snapping turtle or a large water snake. These guys will bite under the water, so care must be taken to stay away from their business end. In this case, work your way carefully back to the tail before you grab hold. If you've grabbed hold of a water snake, this is when the stick I mentioned comes into play.

Before I continue I must tell you the common water snake is one of the nastiest, meanest snakes around. They never become manageable pets. They omit a foul odor and will give you a vicious bite any chance they get. One particular five-footer I had in my collection had managed to escape. He set up a residence in the woodpile by the side of my house. On warm days, he would leave the wood pile and go into my neighbor's yard. When my poor neighbor attempted to chase it away the snake would attack. This went on for some time before I was finally able to recapture the darn thing.

Anyway, back to where I left off. Work your fingers down along the snake until you come to the tail, then grab hold. Begin to quickly turn yourself in a circle swinging the snake and keeping the head away from your body. If you have an assistant have him get the stick ready. Otherwise you will have to grab it with your free hand.

Pin the snake down to the ground with the stick. Try pinning as close as you can to his head. This part gets tricky, because you must now grab the snake just behind the head or else he will bite you. Good luck! If you have read this, Congratulations! You are now a certified Swamper.

Chapter 51 *Sound of Music*

The 60's was a time for music. Folk music had gained wide popularity, and bands like Peter, Paul and Mary and the Kingston trio were topping the charts. One of my favorite teachers had gotten several of his students together and formed a folk band.

They had gotten a couple of gigs up-state at a few clubs. I always loved to listen when they practiced, wishing that I knew how to play a guitar. Sometimes I would sing along as they played. For some reason, this teacher contacted my folks and suggested they get me a microphone. Not knowing anything about this sort of thing, they gave the teacher money to purchase one for me for my birthday.

The music industry was changing fast enough to make your head spin. What would be referred to as 'The British Invasion' had started. The culture of the young people in Willow Creek was also beginning to change.

The days of Fabian, Bobby Darin, Frankie Avalon, Spin the Bottle, drive-ins and make out parties were now becoming things of the past. The Beatles, the Rolling Stones and a few other groups like the Troggs were holding claim to popularity. But there was also a new up-welling of local bands that started to make their mark on the charts. The Rascals, Four Seasons, Zombies, and many others were finding their way to the top ten. The California sound of the Beach Boys and Jan & Dean were also very popular.

By the late 60's many of these music styles began to melt into each other. With all the racial unrest and protest of the draft and the war in Vietnam, some of the fast slipping folk groups found new life in college protest songs at recording studios. Bob Dylan and Phil Ochs' popularity at the collages put them back into the charts. Rock bands like Crosby Stills Nash & Young and The Byrd's started encasing protest into their songs as well, quoting the words from one song by Bob Dylan, "The Times They Are A-changing."

I can recall one particular student in our high school in Willow Creek. His hair was long, almost shoulder length. He wore the strangest looking color-coordinated clothes and shoes. He was given the nickname Surfer Joe, for the lack of any other way to describe his appearance. Most people looked at him as one very strange fella.

Who would have believed that he was a mirror for a style that would become the norm within just a few years? He was mod before anyone even knew what it was. Funny how people laughed at him for his appearance, only to try and look just like him in the very near future. He was also a gifted artist, and I heard he found some fame with his drawings in the days that followed after high school.

The Beatles popularity hit our town like a runaway train. I can still recall the day we all combed our hair down in a mop style worn by this new favorite group. Although our hair was somewhat short, we all did our best to try and capture the Beatles look. Our principal and all the teachers went crazy lining us all up against the hallway wall. They insisted we all put the part back in our hair stating that this was inappropriate dress for school. Boy, if they only knew what was coming just around the corner.

This was the beginning of the local basement or garage band. Music was starting to go on an uncontrolled collision course with itself. Rock, Folk, Pop, Blues even Country were all crashing into each other. Once the smoke cleared, what we were left with was the sound of our generation. I'm not sure what caused so many of us to start up bands, but at one point you could walk down the street where I lived on and hear guitars and drums blasting on almost every block.

This strange phenomenon was noticed by the major TV networks. The Baby Boomers as they are currently referred to, were spinning far more turntables than TV tuners. FM radio stations were also raking in a large share of this music minded generation. Networks would have to come up with a way to pull us back. Some of my friends started jamming together and suggested we put together a band of our own. We had a friend who lived up the street who was a drummer. I took out the microphone that my music teacher had gotten for me and we started our band.

Now it was just a coincidence that there was a family who lived up the street from us whose father worked for one of the major TV networks. He had been given an assignment to do a special on the rise of the Basement or Garage bands. Our band was contacted for a part in the special. Fame was already knocking at our door. We worked as hard as we could to get several songs down tight for the show, and finally received our date for the film shoot.

Suddenly everything came crashing down around me. Our vacation reservation had been planned for the same week as the film shoot. My first big shot at fame had just flown out the window. Our band did do the interview, although I personally never got the chance to watch it. The guys said it went well, but nothing more ever came from the airing of the program.

By 1965, television networks started airing more music-based programming. There was one show in particular that was based on the older Dick Clark's show, American Bandstand. The show featured many of the best American and British acts of the time, also spotlighting new rising stars.

The reason I bring this up is because although my dreams of fame had somehow slipped through my fingers, there was another local group of my friends from the other side of Willow Creek that seemed about to make it big. This had all come about with the help of one of our own Willow Creek teachers. He was known as somewhat of a world traveler.

I can still recall how on one particular occasion the entire school was sent to the auditorium to watch a film of a trip his family had taken to Europe. The film showed many famous places such as the Eiffel Tower and Notre Dame. We found it to be interesting, although several of my friends and I couldn't help but wonder why we never saw our teacher in any of the film footage. Eventually we all just agreed that he must have been the only one to operate the camera.

Anyway, somehow it seemed this teacher had contacts in the entertainment business. After choosing one of our local garage bands I have previously mentioned, he began a promotional campaign for the band.

I remember how every Friday the band members would get out of school early in order for them to fly out to California. They all were wearing the same outfit that distinguished the group. Boy was I envious of those guys. The entire school was very excited to have one of the local bands making it to the big time.

They even put on a special concert for the school and that was really cool. The band got their spot on the Action TV show, and it appeared they were on their way to fame and fortune. But something strange was going on in the background of all this excitement.

In between classes some of us would hang out in the boy's room, sometimes taking a few puffs from a cigarette. On two of these occasions, the teacher I've spoken to you about entered the bathroom. The first time he grabbed me by the back of my neck and lead me out. This seemed strange because teachers never touched the students. The next time he again grabbed me by the back of my neck, but this time he threatened to put my head in the urinal if he caught me in the bathroom again.

At that point I decided to mention what had happened to my folks. They told me to try and stay clear of the teacher and there was to be no more hanging out in the boy's room. As far as I was concerned that was that, I just went about my business. What I didn't know was the fact that my parents had brought this information to the attention of the school board.

Now by this time some of the parents of the band members were starting to become concerned. It seemed that the teacher had taken a considerable amount of money from them under the ruse that it was needed to put the band over the top. As things seemed to slowly come to a halt with the band, their concerns grew. The school started to look closer into the teacher's credentials.

I can't even imagine the shock when they realized he actually was not a teacher at all. His papers were fake, and he was an impostor. He was quickly arrested, and that was the end of the band's career. Sadly, some of the parents got stung for a fairly large amount of cash. After that, not much more was heard about the whole incident until the day one of my friends did a strange thing. He decided to take a corvette from a local dealer for a joy ride. He was always a bit crazy, and this was one of his best stunts ever. The cops chased him through several towns before he finally pulled over. When they placed him in lockup, he was shocked to see his teacher in the next cell. We all had a good laugh after hearing that story.

It wouldn't be till years later that I would bring up the subject of the teacher's abusive behavior with some of the band members. It seems they all had a similar problem, only on a larger scale. I guess it was a good thing they caught this guy when they did. Still, I can't help but wonder if after finally getting out of jail, he decided to change his profession. Maybe he was working in some small town somewhere in the Midwest practicing law or medicine. Just a thought!

Chapter 52 *Always to Young*

It's kind of odd the way time can play games with people. My own personal observation about this phenomenon makes me tend to place our lives into several distinct categories. The first of these I will refer to is the early stage.

During this part of life's journey, the future does not exist. What matters is our present need. If we're hungry, food makes us content. Wet diaper when changed, makes life good. There is no thought of tomorrow during this early time. Only things that fulfill our immediate needs have any meaning or importance at this particular stage of our development.

Not long after this a change occurs as we start to wonder. "Why haven't they given me food yet?" Or, "I don't like the way this stuff tastes!" And, "I think there is a monster in that closet!" We've now entered into the next part of the cycle of life. This is when things suddenly start to become more complicated.

As a boy growing up in a small town for some reason I always found myself too young for just about everything I took an interest in. It seemed that no matter what the task, the answer from my parents was always the same. "To young! Not old enough! When you're older!" blah blah blah. "Jeff can stay out and play after dark! Johnny rides his bike to school! Butch watches that show every Saturday night! Why does it always seem like I'm the only one in Willow Creek that's never old enough?"

I can still recall the way things used to be at the place I worked. Remembering the words my boss would often say to the other workers or a customer. "Get the kid to sweep the floor, or the kid will carry that for you." Always finding myself to be the new kid on the block. The helper on the job site.

Funny how when we're young we find ourselves constantly wishing to be older. "Next year I'm going to be able to do this and that!" Never realizing we're constantly wishing our lives away. Soon enough we find ourselves toiling throughout the week just trying to get to Friday nights and the weekend. This hurry-up process continues through a good part of midlife till suddenly one day we realize something has changed.

The people you work with start turning to you for advice. There seems to never be enough time in the day to finish. Not working becomes a problem because jobs keep piling up and as I used to say. "I'm going to need a vacation to recover from all the work I had to catch up on after my vacation!" This subtle change signals the beginning of the next part of life's journey. Now as I have found myself in the autumn season of my life, I try to find as much time as I can to stop and smell the roses.

Although I've long since left that small town of my youth, I often recall those early days when time seemed to never move fast enough. If I only knew then what I have long since come to realize that some of the most precious moments of my life actually occurred during those early slow-moving days of my youth, growing up in the town of Willow Creek.

Chapter 53 *Opening Day*

There were two special days that I can recall as a youngster. No, I'm sure it's not what you're thinking. Christmas, Birthdays, or Halloween. They were all indeed special to me, but they are not what I would like talk about today. Each of the days that I plan to speak of earmark an important part of the cycle of life. The first of these comes with the beginning of spring. The second day marks the beginning of fall, reminding us all that there is a long sleep of winter which is all too quickly approaching.

Birth and death are the inevitable parts of life. Spring and fall are the seasons in which they are mirrored. The special day I'd like to tell you about today comes at the beginning of spring, or what I call the first season. You see, at this time of the year winter snows begin to melt from the landscapes. Rivers begin to once again flow full to their banks, signaling the beginning of the time of new life, or what most of us refer to as spring. For a young boy growing up in Willow Creek, spring can only mean one thing. The opening day of trout season.

I wouldn't be getting much sleep. For a week or so I had been checking the river every chance I got. I was scouting for the best places to fish on opening day, trying to figure out which pool held the most trout. I always kept a sharp watch out for the big ones.

I had gone over my tackle a million times. New line on my pole, drag perfectly set. Plenty of hooks and sinkers. Worms in the refrigerator, salmon eggs and spinners in my creel. My waders had been checked for holes and then set by the back door. I was ready. Even though all this preparation had started way in advance of the actual event, they would all be needed in order to be ready for this special day. Still no sleep would come to me tonight. I would open the bail of my reel, pick up the line with my index finger, each time making a perfect cast. The fishing line would suddenly tighten and quickly I would set the hook. This always woke me from my sleep, over and over again. Each time I would sit up in bed checking the alarm clock on my nightstand, only to see that just another half hour had passed. Finally, this restless night would end with the buzzing sound of my alarm clock which had been preset for four-thirty. Grabbing the worms and an apple from the fridge, slipping on my waders, I headed for the door. By five o'clock I was peddling my bike hard heading for the river, hoping I had left the house early enough to beat the crowd to my spot. You see opening day of trout season in Willow Creek was a major event. Cars were already parked on the shoulder of the road that ran parallel to the creek.

Laying my bike up against the chain linked fence that ran down to the edge of the stream, I headed for my spot. At this place the river took a sudden horseshoe turn. The bank on the outside of this bend was much higher than the one on the opposite shore. Tree roots had been exposed as the water eroded the soil away during times when the river ran high. Water ran deeper on this bank, so I had decided this was the spot I would start to fish. No one else had gotten to the big bend so I was able to get the best position on the bank. Soon the river would be full of fishermen standing shoulder to shoulder. They would all be nervously checking their watches for the magic time when we all could begin fishing. (Eight O'clock!)

After checking to see how fast the river was running, I decided to place one small split shot sinker on the line for weight. Two salmon eggs on a small hook was what I was going to start with for bait. As I rested my pole up against a large tree at the edge of the bank, fishing line hanging down roughly a foot or so from the tip of my fishing pole, I was ready.

Two salmon eggs swung back and forth in the breeze like the pendulum on an old clock as I checked my Timex watch which showed two minutes to eight. If I had set the time right this was it. Closely watching the other fishermen, I was like a caged tiger. The second their line hit the water so would mine.

After I fished for an hour or so, I decided it was time to start working my way down the river, fishing under each of the bushes that hung out over the river's bank. I would always keep a watchful eye out for large boulders in the water that could create pools or eddy's that might hold fish. There was just one small problem with my plan. In order to continue making my way down stream, I would have to cross this one farm field. This field belonged to one of the nastiest, meanest mules I have ever known. The two of us were by no means strangers to each other. This animal had chased me across this field many times. His intent was to take a large chunk out of this young boy's backside. It seemed that this day would be no different. There he stood in the center of the hay field just waiting and watching for me to make my move. Something was not quite the same. As I started to make my way across the field, the mule made no move, instead just stood there. I was keeping a close watch out from the corner of my eye, not wanting to make direct eye contact with that crazy animal. I got half way across the field moving toward the safety of the woods, and still the mule just stood there watching. Could this be the first time he wouldn't charge? My wishful thoughts were suddenly dashed when the beast started to stomp his right front hoof throwing puffs of dust in the air. This was it! I had no doubt the mule was ready to launch his attack. Quickly I started to sprint for the trees. That's when I realized there was no chance of escape. This demon animal was on me in a flash.

Now I guess you could call it fate that as I was preparing to be bitten, I happened to notice the broken branch lying on the ground by my feet. As quickly as I could I picked up the stick and faced my attacker. The mule's teeth were snapping wildly, froth flying from its mouth as it was about to take its first bite. Pure panic came over me as I swung the stick at the mule.

What happened next would come as a total shock. The crazed animal suddenly backed off from his charge. Still not feeling safe, I lifted the branch once more and waited for my enemy to make a move. Once again, the mule shied. That's when the light bulb went on in my head. This animal had never been stood up to before. I was always running away from the darn beast. This day everything was about to change. Swinging the branch wildly and yelling, I started my own attack. The mule turned and fled back to the safety of the far side of his field. From that day forward all fear was lost crossing that hay field, as long as I carried a big stick.

My life lesson that came from this day was you should never run from a bully. If you stand up to him, he will probably stand down to you. If not, it's still better to deal with trouble than the run from it. Also, it's just not worth carrying fear around in your back-pocket cause there could be a mule ready to take a chunk from that general proximity.

Chapter 54 *Absentee*

From the time I had turned sixteen till the year I graduated high school, a few of my friends and I were plagued with a strange type of illness. It always started around the same time during the fall, as the morning air began to chill, coating our lawns with what looked like white sugar crystals. We all began to suffer the same strange symptoms. Our concentration started to falter. Our homework assignments were incomplete, and generally we all became very poor students.

Each year our parents would be forced to turn in the same note to our principal concerning this strange disease. We were always considered absent due to illness. This sickness would spread across the small rural towns of America affecting so many young students that in some towns it became necessary to close school altogether. After some close examination of this virus, it would finally be isolated, named and all school principals notified. It was known as the opening day of 'Hunting Season.'

Sorry to bounce you all around the table like that, but in many places in the country it really was somewhat of a problem. My friends and I did in fact turn in the same (due to illness) absence excuse every year. This is the second favorite time of the year that I have previously mentioned. Once my friends and I turned sixteen, we had to take a Hunter's Safety Course. Our instructor was a conductor on the Erie Railroad. He was an avid hunter who was eager to teach us the ways of the woods. He showed us the proper method to clean and care for our guns. How to shoot, and most importantly, the safety procedures for carrying guns in the field. By the time we walked out into the woods we had many hours of safety training drummed into our heads.

Back when I was young, a hunting license was much more simplified than it is today. As I recall all game basically fell under one state hunting permit. We were not very knowledgeable about deer hunting in those early days, so squirrel, rabbit and game birds were our main targets. Mom always did her best to cook up these critters I brought home for table fare. I don't know if she had ever been exposed to wild game before I started hunting. Squirrel can look mighty scary when it is plopped into a frying pan with butter and onions. If she was disturbed about it, she never let on.

There was one particular game bird we loved to hunt. It had the ability to fly faster than a man's eye could focus. The only warning a hunter gets when he flushes out one of these birds is the beating drum-like sound just before the bird takes to flight.

This bird I speak of is known as a Ruffed Grouse. Grouse take a straight away flight pattern, flying low and extremely fast, making them one of the toughest birds to hit. On the other hand, the Woodcock, another type of game bird we hunted, flew in a corkscrew-like circular pattern, usually rising ten to fifteen feet upward before it began its escape. By the time you pressed the trigger the crazy bird was somewhere else. More times than I can recall, my success with these birds came by shooting where the bird hadn't gotten to yet rather than attempting to hit the actual target. Sad but today Grouse have all but vanished from the area. Some claim it's because of the land development of brush and timber areas that the bird requires for its existence. Others blame all the DDT spraying that went on for years. The truth probably takes in all the above and more to cover the explanation, but these birds are now sadly few and far between.

Anyway, if your son or daughter suddenly seems ill as the first leaves begin to fall and the chilling wind from the north starts to blow, take out your pen and start writing their 'due to illness' excuse and consider yourself lucky because they are heading out into nature. They are breathing fresh air and getting exercise rather than sitting by a tv or computer screen.

Chapter 55 *Draft*

Time for graduating from high school had suddenly come upon us. Talk of proms and parties seemed to be all that was on the minds of our graduating class at Willow Creek. We were finally going to be free from what we considered all the teachers' dumb rules. No more books or homework assignments. This was going to be the best time of our lives! Or was it?

They called me in to see the school guidance counselor. The woman looked over my records for a few moments, then she glanced over the top of her glasses. "Well, what are you planning to do with your life?" This question hit me like a train and I didn't have a clue. "Your grade average doesn't look too good for college. Have you given any thought to learning a trade?" The fact of the matter was I really hadn't given any thought to anything at all about my future. I was too busy chasing girls, driving fast cars and drinking at bars! My parents also started to apply this same kind of pressure at home. I would not find any peace until I was able to come up with some kind of career game plan. Even if it was something I made up just to get everyone off my back. The trouble was that back in the late 1960's the war in South Indochina had escalated. If you were a young man between eighteen and twenty-five you were at high risk of being drafted.

My school counselor informed me that I could avoid the draft if I went to college and was able to maintain a B-average. "Yep, well good luck with that," I said to myself. I was lucky that I was able to finally graduate from high school. Now I must say, I really had no interest in going to fight a war in some far-off country that I had only recently heard of for reasons that seemed totally unclear. This whole conflict was being protested throughout the country, and some young people were actually running up to Canada to avoid the draft. My dad had been somewhat quiet lately about this matter. Dinner table discussions about Vietnam were a topic our family usually avoided. My father would flip out when he heard news about the protesters and draft dodgers, but on my eighteenth birthday something changed. As I have mentioned earlier my father had started drinking on the way home from work. Something had been bothering him but what it was seemed unclear. It had become a ritual for a friend of mine and I to meet early every Sunday morning at the local Chocolate Shop. The newspaper would be dropped off outside the store well before it opened. We would clip one of the string ties that held the paper bundle together and slide out one of the papers. We were checking to see where we stood in the draft. On this particular Sunday both my friend's birthday and mine appeared in the paper. This was it, we were about to be drafted. That night at dinner I gave my parents the news. Dad was quiet for a while, then he began to speak. "I went through hell in the war, so you would never have to! There is no way that I'm going to let you sleep in a fox hole. If you have to join you are either going into the Navy or the Air Force. I have a friend who is a recruiter, I will speak with him and see what he can do."

Both my friend and I agreed that the Air Force sounded good if we were to have a choice. Dad had arranged an appointment for us with his recruiter friend, and after filling out a ton of paperwork there was nothing left to do but wait. After a week or so a letter arrived at the homes of my friend and I informing us to report to a place in New York City called White Hall. This was to be for our indoctrination into the Air Force.

White Hall as I recall was a large corner brown-stone. When we entered the building, there was a spiraling staircase which took you up through the heart of the building. I can recall looking down over the rail to get a better view. You could see each floor straight down to the first-floor lobby. The building built in 1884 was indeed a unique corner peace of real estate. There was a bird cage type elevator. The door was made of elaborately structured iron bars. Moving from floor to floor everything was open to view. We weren't too comfortable with that old elevator so both of us used the stairs. As fate would have it, we would turn out to be some of the last young men to go through White Hall. Not long after, the building was bombed in protest to the war, never to reopen again.

Anyway, let me get back to our day. I still remember how cold it was in that old building. We were ordered to strip down to our shorts. There were around thirty of us standing there in our underwear shivering, packed tightly in this cold room like a can of sardines. At this point we were all informed by a recruiter holding a toothbrush in his hand that they were able to hold us for 48 hours. So, if anyone had tried to tamper with their blood pressure or had taken drugs, they would find themselves scrubbing the floor with the brush he was holding until the time that they could be retested.

Next, they drew blood from us. We all carried the full test tubes of our blood as we walked around from room to room being poked and prodded for what seemed like hours. By the time I got to the last doctor, I was about to pass out from looking at that damn test tube. Shots always made me squeamish when I was young. The doctor told me to have a seat for a few minutes. He smiled and told me not to worry "You should see the Asian kids. They all drop like flies!" Somehow this made me feel somewhat better.

After all was done they lined us up. A soldier walked down the line pointing at each one of us as he announced: "Regular Army, regular Army, regular Army, Marines." My friend and I held our breath as they approached us. All I could think of was that there was going to be a mistake and 'Marines' was what I was about to hear. As it turned out we were the only two 'Air Force' in the room. Then we all raised our right hand and were sworn into service. My friend and I had taken a 90-day delayed enlistment. This left us the entire summer to sow some wild oats before we had to report. There was a tv show called Route 66. It was about two young guys traveling across country in a convertible Corvette. We didn't have a Corvette, but my friend did have a convertible Corvair. We both had made the decision that we would spend that summer driving cross country to California.

Getting the Corvair Ready for Our Road Trip

Chapter 56 *Road Trip*

Camping gear, check, maps check, Travelers Checks check, cash check. We packed the Corvair with everything we could think of that might be needed on our cross-country trip. We both had a strange feeling about this journey. Neither of us knew what the future would bring. The thought that in a few months we might be fighting, or worse killed, haunted both of us. The saying 'Eat and drink for tomorrow we die' had suddenly become a real possibility. This was to be our summer to experience all we could, in case it turned out to be our last.

Several years prior to this trip I had traveled cross country with my family. I remembered several places that I felt were worth revisiting. This helped us map out our course. The first hold-over stop I recall was at a KOA campground at a place in Wisconsin called the Dells. The land by the campground was an Indian Reservation. There was a large river that ran through this area. Because of the way this river ran, it had cut deep gorges along its banks, and was often referred to as the little Grand Canyon. We both decided to try and do some fishing that evening. We had no bait, so we decided to use some hot dogs. Somewhere along the way we had picked up a gallon jug of wine. Fish or no fish, we were going to have a fun evening. It didn't take long before we had the first run on one of our lines.

Neither of us had ever seen a channel catfish before. We couldn't believe the large size of these angry fish. To this day, fishing for channels at night is still one of my favorite pastimes. Anyway, the last hookup we had that night snapped forty-pound Dacron line. I was never able to turn the fish whatever it was. If you like fishing and you manage to find yourself in Wisconsin, give the Dells a try. The two of us polished off that gallon of wine and staggered back to the campground. We wouldn't get underway the next day till late afternoon. Our next planned stop was in the Black Hills of South Dakota. I had remembered that there was some really good trout fishing in a lot of the lakes and streams.

We stopped at a small sports shop to see if we

could purchase licenses. That was when something caught our attention. As we spoke to the store owner we started looking at the glass counter in front of us. There was a large number of various types of handguns. "You boys want take a look?" Now we both had just finished telling the store owner about the fact that we were going into the service. For some reason we thought, what the heck, we were now in the military and we should both have guns. The fella behind the counter informed us that there was a forty-eight hour cool down period before you could buy a gun after filing permits. We told him we were not going to be around the area that long. That's when he offered to make a phone call. As it turned out the judge in town was at home doing laundry. "Send the boys over to the house, I'm just getting ready to make breakfast!" He made us coffee and gave us some pastry. We explained about our delayed enlistment and how we had decided to take a cross country trip. You couldn't meet a nicer guy. I believe if there was ever a Mayberry, this was it.

The judge signed our papers and handed them

back to us. "You boys leave those guns in the boxes. Put them in the trunk of your car until tomorrow. After that you load them and keep them on the seat of your car in plain sight." We thanked the judge, and after picking up our guns headed on our way. I guess you could now consider us armed and dangerous.

Chapter 57 *My Companion*

Before I continue my story, I feel I should tell you a little about my traveling partner. He stood somewhere around five foot-three inches tall, always well-groomed, keeping his hair perfectly combed and his face always close-shaven. This clean appearance gave one the impression that he was someone who would never cause trouble. That's why you should never judge a person by the way they look!

You see, in spite of his smallish size my friend was endowed with an Irish temper. His seemingly good nature could change in an instant, causing him to go off like a roman candle. He never picked a fight with someone his own size, instead It seemed he always managed to find the biggest guy in the place to have an altercation with. This was always a concern to yours truly, not wanting to get my head busted open in some senseless bar brawl.

On one particular occasion, several of our acquaintances were sitting with us at a table in a bar. This one particular fella with us, was as big as a house.

Something was wrong with one of his eyes causing it to look in a different direction than the other. Everyone called him Snake. Now Snake was a nice enough guy when he was sober, but if he was drinking he had the ability to tear an establishment apart. I had watched him in action in brawls numerous times and had no wish to cross his path.

This night we were all drinking fairly heavily. I can't say for sure how the argument started between my friend and Snake. All I remember was my buddy suddenly cracking a beer bottle over this big guys head. "Damn!" I shouted at my friend in sudden panic. Snake didn't seem to have sustained any serious damage at all from the blow, although he did seem somewhat disoriented. Grabbing my friend, we quickly headed for the door before Snake's mind cleared. As I recall this was the first time both of Snakes eyes seemed to look in the same direction.

This was the temperament of my traveling companion. Fortunately, the guy we called Snake suffered no serious damage from that beer bottle and both my friend and I would sit with him many times after that incident. I don't believe the big guy even remembered being clocked in the head. So anyway, now you've met my traveling companion.

Chapter 58 *Blue Mounds*

Next stop on our road trip was a place in Minnesota called Blue Mounds. We had arrived at the park late and the admissions office was already closed for the night. We left our information in a drop box at the entrance, then entered into the park in search of a place to set up our tent. The place seemed relatively empty that evening as we drove around the grounds. Maybe it was due to the fact that we had arrived at the park in the middle of the week.

I had visited this park several years before with my family. One of the main points of interest in the park was a giant cliff. It was used by the Native American tribes to capture buffalo. A buffalo jump as it was called, is a place that was used to stampede a herd forcing them to jump off a cliff. Using this method, a tribe could quickly kill a large number of animals. Enough food for the entire tribe. Anyway, after we set up our tent in the pitch black of night we managed to polish off a couple of six packs of beer, then we both went to sleep. I can't say for sure what time it was when we were awakened by the sound of the train. Tired from our day's long travel and a bit foggy from all the beer we had consumed, we simply noted that the damn thing was loud. Neither of us had noticed rail tracks as we had entered the park, but that train was really close. Once the rumbling passed we both pulled our sleeping bags up over our heads and quickly fell back to sleep. It wasn't long after we were both once again awakened. This time instead of a train it was the bright blinding glare of spot lights and loud shouts that pulled us from our sleep.

"Are you folks alright?" came voices from outside our tent. "What the hell!" I said to myself as I started to crawl out of my sleeping bag. It was what happened next that totally shook me from my slumber. My air mattress started to move as I reached out trying to place my hand on the tent floor. There was a cold wet feeling on my arm. It seemed that the two of us were both floating in around four to six inches of water. We shouted back at the voices outside the tent that we were alright. It seems the train we thought we heard had actually been a tornado. It had torn right through the middle of the park just missing us by a quarter of a mile or so. It took us a good part of the day to dry out all our gear before we could move on. All the time laughing about how lucky we had been that night and wondering what would have happened if we had set up camp on the other side of the park. Or if that damn thing had taken a slightly different path. It seems the simple decisions we make each day can have a profound effect on the rest of our lives.

Chapter 59 *The Path Less Traveled*

It's my belief that there is just one key factor that drives a person to suddenly pull off the expressway and begin to travel the backroads. What some refer to as 'the path less traveled'.

Time! Time controls most of our lives. We hurry to go to work on time then we rush to get back home. When we're young we want time to pass quickly so we will be old enough to do all the things older kids can do. We're always looking for the fastest route to get from one place to another.

Basically, most of us are constantly attempting to rush our lives away. If a person is very fortunate they may find themselves no longer pressed by the need to arrive. It becomes the journey that matters, not the time of arrival at your destination. Hence, we exit and take the road less traveled. There is another reason why one might suddenly pull off life's highway. It's because they have suddenly discovered that they are actually running out of time. At this point some become more interested in the 'living' than in the 'getting there'.

We were somewhere in Montana when we decided to fold up the maps, slipping them back behind the passenger seat as we took the exit. I'm not sure if the decision to leave the highway was made because we still had over a month left before we had to report for our deployment, or if we were both just so unsure of what our futures held. Whichever the reason, we both felt the need to travel to a place that was not marked by a triangle on a map. For two northern boys the open spaces of these western states was something that we just couldn't get used to. Vast, wide-open land for as far as the eye could see. Ranches so large that it took an airplane to see where the property lines might be.

Makes a person from the north wonder why we live all bunched up under such crowded conditions. Not really knowing exactly what we were looking for, we decided to just keep driving until we found it. Whatever it was. It was getting late in the day and we were thinking that it was time to find a place to pitch our tent.

That's when we noticed this guy on his John Deere tractor. I told my partner to pull over, so we could talk to him. After our introductions we asked the rancher if there was a place we could put up our tent for a day or so. This rancher was extremely gracious, he offered to take us down the road around a mile to his grandfather's original ranch house. I believe these folks in the more rural areas of this country still stood up for patriotism. They did not like what was going on with the antiwar movement and the hippy protesters. So just like the judge we met up in the Black Hills, after telling the rancher about our military plans he became very willing to help. We asked him if it would be alright if we did some shooting. Both of us were itching to fire those pistols we had purchased in the Dakotas. He told us that there was no closed season on jackrabbits, so we could have at it.

This old, long abandoned ranch house looked like something right out of a western movie. There was an old windmill that was used to draw water. Now as the wind blew against the old wooden paddles they creaked and groaned. The ranch house was very small unlike the massive building and commercial barns of the current owner. There were old shutters hanging loosely from the windows. As the wind pushed against them they would smack the clapboard siding. This place reminded us of an old western ghost town.

A hog pen was attached to the side of the house. There were still four massive sows in the pen. We couldn't believe how large these animals were. Having hogs so close to the house must have been rough on the sinuses during the heat of summer. Anyway, this was to be our home for the next few days. After setting up camp, we loaded our six guns and hit the dusty trail. I guess what I'm trying to say is that we found ourselves totally caught up in our surroundings. This old ranch made us feel like we had returned to the days of the old west. Now being that we were both northern boys, neither of us had ever seen a jack rabbit and figured we wouldn't know the difference when we did. To us rabbits were rabbits and out here in the west they were all just varmints.

As we crossed over the top of this ridge that was located not far from the ranch, neither of us were prepared for what we were about to see. At first, I thought it was a deer, no, maybe it is and antelope. The two of us stood there looking back and forth at each other trying to figure out what this thing was and if we should shoot. Finally, my buddy lifted his gun and cocked the hammer back. I decided this was it and did the same.

The two of us opened fire and the hombre fell. Imagination can be a funny thing if you let it take you. For a short time, I was back in the days of Tombstone, fighting the outlaws at the OK Corral. We each managed to get a jackrabbit that day. After posing for pictures with our catch, we hung the rabbits up on the hog pen fence trying to decide if we should roast them over the fire or cut them up for stew. Neither of us new for sure if folks ate these things or not. "Maybe we should see if we could find the rancher and ask him," I said. Thinking that was a good idea, we headed for the car when we heard the crunching noise coming from the hog pen. Looking back over at the fence, we noticed both our rabbits were gone. As we approached the pen we couldn't believe what we saw. Those hogs were eating our entire catch.

They were crunching on the rabbit's bones like they were potato chips. Never had either of us ever given any thought to the fact those old pigs could have actually been dangerous. All I can say is don't ever mess around near a hog pen. Those nasty animals will kill you and eat you whole in a heartbeat. Oh well, so much for our dinner idea.

This is when more trouble was about to start. We reloaded our guns, and after scouting the hills around the ranch we failed to find any more jacks. But as we returned to camp we spotted the cotton-tail. It seems that there were several of these smaller rabbits living in the brush around the back of the old ranch house.

So, after stalking around a bit we managed to shoot three more rabbits. That's when the rancher pulled up in his truck. "You boys been doing an awful lot of shooting! What you get?" When we lifted up our catch, the rancher's smile suddenly faded. "You boys know there's a season for Cotton Tails?! I guess we won't get any around here this year." Man, I have to tell you we really felt dumb. Unfortunately, the damage had already been done and the rancher said it would be best that we moved on.

After breaking down our camp, we climbed into the Corvair and continued up the road on our journey. We both felt really bad for being so ignorant about the hunting laws in Montana. That rancher was very kind to allow us to use his grandfather's old place. I'll always remember how cool it was feeling like we had gone back in time to the days of the old wild west. Unfortunately, as in my telling of this story I also remember how stupid we both were. Oh well, I guess hopefully we learn from our mistakes.

My First Jack

Chapter 60 *Mountain Lion*

We would have another shot at reliving the days of the old west somewhere out in Wyoming before we headed for the City of Angels. I can't recall how we actually made friends with these two guys, but their father also owned a large ranch. Needless to say, we all hit it off pretty good, and after some small talk and a couple of beers we all decided to go hunting.

No small game hunting this time. There had been a cougar spotted in the area. The boys knew that their dad wouldn't mind if we went looking for that damn cat. The two of us were very excited about the possibility of getting a shot at a mountain lion. This trip would be done on horseback. Our new-found friends asked if we were any good at riding. I was not familiar with horses at all and although totally excited about this hunting trip, sadly I was forced to admit that this was one cowboy who had never been on a horse. Our new friends both laughed. "Put him on the black," the one fella said to the other as they headed into the stable to saddle the horses.

The horse they had chosen for me seemed older than the other three. As my friends started to move, my horse just calmly followed along. This made me glad because I had no idea how I was supposed to steer this animal. The group was always stopping in order for me to catch up. This was a little embarrassing for me, but at least for the most part the black horse knew exactly what it was doing. Riding across the open prairie is an incredible experience. Once again, we were sent back in time to the days of the old west. At one spot we all stopped in order to watch a dust funnel spout cut across the open land out in front of us. These small dust tornadoes occur quite often on the open prairie and are fascinating to watch. This ranch we were visiting was close to the foothills. It didn't take long before the flat, vast open space suddenly changed into an ocean of what seemed like a never-ending rolling waves of hilly landscape.

Although my horse did well when we crossed the

flats, taking me down hill was an altogether new experience. Basically, I was holding on for dear life each time we made our way down into another gulch, as the cowboys called it. Unfortunately, we saw no sign of mountain lions that day. We did a lot of target practice, each of us taking turns with the pistols and rifles we were carrying. The day passed quickly and soon it was time for us to return back to the ranch. This was when something totally unexpected occurred.

The rancher's sons that we were hunting with suggested that we all race back to the ranch. "Oh boy!" I said to myself, "this horse I'm riding was last all day. I'm thinking I'll probably end up lost out in this darn prairie." Needless to say, in the true western spirit, whoops and yahoo's could be heard across the plains as our horses blew through clouds of prairie dust.

Now I will never know if what happened next was planned by these boys or just something that had been overlooked. My old, black, lazy horse suddenly seemed to wake up, exploding like it had been shot from a cannon. I held on for dear life as this crazy animal seemed to fly across the prairie. Looking back over my shoulder I could just barely make out my friends. "Oh mamma!" No idea where this animal was taking me or what its plans were. I was starting to think it wants to kill me for sure and it has been waiting all day for just the right chance. All I could do was close my eyes and hold on. The next time my eyes opened the horse stable was in plain sight. Lucky me, I guess this horse knew exactly where it wanted to go. Maybe it was fed up carrying this dumb greenhorn around all day. It seemed like ten minutes or more would pass before the rest of the hunting party found its way back to the stable. The boys' father was not at all happy about the heated condition of our horses. Both of them were in big trouble, and we were once again asked to leave. Although on this particular occasion I take no responsibility for our trouble. That black demon I was sitting on was the one who deserves all the credit.

Chapter 61 *Vegas*

Nevada was going to be our next planned holdover stop for a few days. The Corvair had been giving us a bit of trouble due to the desert heat. The car had a rear, air-cooled engine which when exposed to high heat would develop something called vapor lock, which caused it to stall. We had quickly learned that although the car used no water, we were still forced to carry a full Jerry can.

It seemed the only way to break the vapor lock was to pour water over a certain breather vent located on the engine's side. This had happened to us a few times in the mountains heading into Las Vegas. If you have ever driven those roads you know how steep and treache-rous they can be. It seemed crazy, but Nevada had no speed limit. We had discovered that when this happened we were able to put the shift in neutral and coast almost all the way down into Vegas. My partner called it 'Jewish overdrive'. We did manage to save a lot on gas using that method.

Finally, we arrived in casino town. One of the first things we noticed as we were coming into town was a lot of guys selling stuff at the road side. Suitcases, clothing, guitars, basically everything they owned. We couldn't help but wonder if these people blew all their money gambling and were trying to make enough to get home. Or could it be that they had become so addicted to the sport that they were hoping to get enough money for one more shot?

The other strange thing about Vegas is the large amount of small wedding chapels and divorce lawyers. I'm sorry, but I just don't get it. Why would anyone go through all the trouble? Just shack up and say the hell with it. Possibly my generation looks at things a little differently than our parents did in the past. We decided to get a hotel room for a day or so, unpacked the car and headed for the heart of town.

The legal age for gambling and alcohol in Vegas was twenty-one. We both fell short by a year or two, so we decided to stay out of the larger casinos where we thought we might get proofed. We looked for street level slot machine parlors. These buildings' sides were wide open to the street. Large, metal garage doors could be pulled down if the place wanted to close, but I don't believe they ever did. It was easy for us to walk in, pull a few levers and then move on without drawing any attention.

A hundred bucks apiece was what we decided to blow. Both of us hoped to score with some girls somewhere along the line. That seemed to be something we both always had on our minds.

My hundred bucks was gone so fast it would make your head spin. I began looking around the place for my partner. Maybe he was having better luck than I had. That's when I spotted the blond waitress crossing the floor caring a few drinks on a small serving tray. My eyes widened as I followed the direction she was heading. I must tell you I've always had a weakness for blondes. I was in hot pursuit as she turned the corner to the next row of slots. There stood my partner with a tray full of quarters. The girl handed him the two drinks and he gave me one. You're not going to believe this he said, just watch! He pulled down the handle on the machine, and what looked like the jelly bean light on a cop's car started flashing red along with a blaring siren and bell. The blonde waitress came back quickly smiling at us. My buddy had somehow managed to empty the slot machine. This forced us to wait till she got this guy to come and refill it, so the machine could finish paying off. We both ordered more drinks from the blonde waitress. When she returned she had a second waitress with her. It was starting to look like our luck had really changed for the better. The girls handed me a bag and suggested I bring the quarters over to the counting machine and cash them in. They told my partner not to move away or he could lose the machine. Each time they refilled the slot machine he pulled the handle and the damn light went off again. We were convinced this slot machine was malfunctioning. The law said you couldn't make someone leave a machine for twenty-four hours. We had cashed in over a grand in quarters when the casino manager approached us.

"I'll need to see some ID from you boys!" he exclaimed. The girls scoffed, "He knew you two probably weren't twenty-one. He didn't care as long as you kept dumping money into the slots!" We had both decided that if we got carded we would come up with some story about how we managed to leave our stuff at the hotel. Thank goodness we had already cashed in most of the coins. The manager booted us both out of the casino. The girls threatened to quit, but we convinced them that it was a bad move. For some reason we never managed to hook up with these two. Nevertheless, we found ourselves back in the Corvair with the hope that maybe we would do better when we got to the city of love, San Francisco.

Chapter 62 *The Culture*

This was a time of many changes in our country. Hippie flower-power or the love generation as some called it, had suddenly taken over the country by a storm. Antiwar protesters, civil rights movement, college unrest, psychedelic drug explosion, a sexual revolution, the draft, the Vietnam war, and other social issues all collided into each other.

'Don't trust anyone over thirty' was a motto many young people lived by. Our parents were old school and didn't understand anything about our new generation. We were all determined to change the world. Somehow? Some took this much wanted change to extremes. Groups like the Weathermen and Black Panthers had armed themselves and were not afraid to use bombs, guns or whatever it took to pursue their cause. Young people were beginning to learn that there was great strength in numbers. If you do something considered illegal you get arrested, but when hundreds do it, you either create a riot or the police just stand and watch. Our generation had learned to use the power of the people. Even our music was based on protest. Bob Dylan, Phil Oaks, Country Joe and the fish, just to mention a few had taken their protest songs directly to the colleges. This was the easy way to unify a cause by bringing it directly to large groups of young people all at one time.

Some of these gatherings would explode in violence but eventually the stand down and observe attitude became the norm. People in positions of government and police started to believe that the unrest in the country was being perpetrated by some type of communist groups. Anyone that was considered a leader of protest no matter what the cause would be investigated.

I can still recall the words to a hit song playing on the radio. 'If you're going to San Francisco, be sure to wear some flowers in your hair.' We were on our way; free love was calling, and many of us wanted to somehow become a part of this new revolution.

Before I continue telling you about our road trip, I

would like to slip back in time to around a year or so. My travelling companion and I had been hanging out at this local bar a good part of the night. It was close to closing time when this guy we knew asked if we were interested in going to a party at his friend's house. I believe what he really wanted was a ride, but no matter it had been a quiet night and we were looking for something to do.

We pulled into a driveway, walked up to the house and knocked at the door. A guy opened the door and the three of us entered. All the lights were out in the house and the first thing we noticed was the strange sweet smell if incense. Candles were burning on several tables and four or five people were lying around the room on the couch and floor. No one was saying much as they made room for us on one of the couches. They were playing some kind of strange music I had never heard before and the whole atmosphere of the room seemed very peculiar. One of the guys took out a bag of what I believe was marijuana. Taking great care, he managed to roll this funny looking cigarette and proceeded to hand it to the three of us. I said thanks, but I had my own, as I pulled a regular butt from my pack.

This was the first time my friend and I had ever been exposed to drugs. Both of us suddenly became very uncomfortable about this whole situation. You see this was a time when the schools had police come to our classroom to teach about drug awareness. They showed us what pot looked like and what a joint was. Told us stories of how one guy was found in closet. He had been in there a week after smoking a joint. They painted a grim picture about the dark side of using marijuana, telling us only one puff could get us hooked. Basically, they were trying to scare the crap out of us. This was a time when even one of the more popular detective shows did a story about a couple who smoked and then carelessly let their daughter drown in the bathtub. It was all really scary, not to mention the criminal aspect of what would happen if you got caught with this stuff in your possession. The two of us decided that we better get the hell out of that house before the cops showed up to break down the door. As we were driving away we both laughed about how strange the people in that house were acting.

Our parents had always done their best to teach us right from wrong, and we usually accepted these things to be totally accurate. For instance, believing that our government was always by the people and for the people. They could not accept the idea that government might become tainted by politicians and large business for personal gain.

Although they meant well, in our opinion what they thought to be true wasn't always exactly correct. Sort of like a celibate priest giving marriage counseling. Sorry for that analogy but I think you will get the point. Young people slowly started to question some of the things they were being taught.

This started a slow rolling ball that continued to gain speed as it traveled downhill. For instance, the anti-drug programs I've mentioned. As more and more young people found themselves doubting what they were being taught about these matters they started to experiment. Very slowly one by one young people started to smoke marijuana. They were finding it to be a pleasant experience. No one locked themselves in the closet or drowned their baby. They found that music sounded better, food tasted better and in general they just were having a good time. No sign of any kind of horrible addiction ever reared its ugly head. To this day it's still referred to as a gateway drug. This may be somewhat true, but not necessarily for the reasons you may think. In late sixties through the early seventies the hippie drug culture went on a rampage. Due to the growing distrust in our older generation, young people decided not to listen to anything coming from their elders. This may be where the drug culture trouble started. Young folks thought that if everyone lied about pot they probably lied about everything else also. It eventually opened the door to experimentation with just about any illegal drug you could think of. At the same time drug companies got into the action. Diet pills, Quaalude, Valium and a whole potpourri of narcotics were flooding into the hippie marketplace.

The prescription sales of these so-called

medications went through the roof. Drug corporate America had become a virtual gold mine. Then to add to all this came a new addition to the drug culture. Something that was called 'psychedelic'.

Chapter 63 *The Bridge*

We had finally reached the farthest destination of
our road trip. Both of us were completely blown away by
the view as we drove over the San Francisco Bay
Bridge. This was it, the place where the hippie culture
had its founding roots. It was indeed strange that the
heart of the 'Love Generation' was a street called
Haight. Anyway, we had finally arrived.

Neither of us had a plan now that we were in the
city. We just started cruising around looking for some
kind of happening. We saw Berkeley College and
Haight-Ashbury and found this one road that would rival
the most extreme roller coaster rides. What we didn't
see were any throngs of young people. In fact, for a big
city the streets seemed almost empty. There was no
hint of what all the songs we'd been hearing on the
radio were talking about. No one wearing flowers in their
hair, no music or protesters, not a hint of anything
unusual about this place. We were getting pretty
disappointed, although the place was interesting it was

just not at all what we had been expecting. We did manage to notice one interesting thing as we cruised around the streets.

On this one corner was a building that caught our attention. If I recall correctly, Barbizon was written over the entrance. Each time we passed we spotted these beautiful models coming in and out of the building. Girls were something that seemed to always be on our minds back in those days, so we kept driving in a circle by the building trying to figure out a way to possibly get to talk to some of the them. Each time as we rounded one particular corner we were aware of this guy standing their waving at us frantically.

My partner finally decided to pull over in order to find out what he wanted. Pulling his pistol out from down under the seat, he set it next to him just before our car pulled to the curb.

This fella approached us with a friendly introduction. "Hi, my name's John! I've been watching you guys pass by this corner a few times and I noticed your plates. What part of the state are you guys from?" When we told him, we lived in the town of Willow Creek, he smiled. "Small world! I'm from the next town over! You want me to show you around the city?" Well he seemed friendly enough, so after we talked with him a bit longer we decided he was okay. Besides, we had no idea what or where we were going.

Strange that as we were traveling we kept running into people from the Willow Creek area. There was a bartender in Park City, Utah. A father and daughter that ran a hunting camp in the Black Hills, and now our new-found tour guide. It's a small world indeed.

Packing our new-found friend into the car we started our tour. The first thing my partner asked him as we started to drive was what was the deal with all the girls we kept seeing coming in and out of that building on the corner. He started laughing telling us "Forget about them. They're all guys!" We both stared at him with a confused look. "What do you mean?" I asked. "They're all transvestites! Boys, welcome to San Francisco." We both looked at each other in total shock.

So much for our plans for possible romance. Unfortunately for us, except for the two waitresses we met at the casino when we got thrown out of Vegas, we hadn't even talked to any girls our entire trip cross country.

We both had big plans for this free love we were hearing about but there was no sign of it here. When we asked what happened to all the 'flower people' we heard about, he informed us that hard drug dealers had moved into the area. Crime had gotten bad and people were getting killed. He said most of the hippies had left the city and headed to Los Angeles. That started both of us thinking that we wouldn't be hanging around this city very long. I turned to the back seat to ask John what he was doing in San Francisco. "I'm a go-fer for a film company. We're shooting some scenes at a local pool hall for a movie with Steve McQueen. My job is to go out and get him anything he wants. I have to stop by the shoot, you want to take a look?" "Sure!" we both agreed "That would be really cool!"

He directed us to a building and told us to park the

car in front. There was a motorcycle cop with a white helmet standing at the entrance to a walk-up pool hall. John waved to him as he opened the door. Seeing this cop had me a little nervous, but John obviously knew him. The three of us entered the building and proceeded to walk up the stairs. The pool room was dark, still we could just barely see the camera set up around the pool table. We watched this guy shooting a few setup shots. John told us that the guy was a famous pool shooter but I'm sorry to say I cannot recall his name. Unfortunately, they weren't shooting anything with McQueen in the shots at that time, so once John took care of some business with one of the guys on the set we left the pool hall.

As we walked down the stairs I asked him what it was he gave to that camera guy. John smiled "Just dropped off a lid for him." "Oh." I replied, not really having any idea what he was talking about. He somehow sensed my ignorance as to what he was saying. "Grass! Part of my job as a go-fer is to get them grass." Now I understood what he was talking about, remembering the party I've previously mentioned where the guys were smoking marijuana or grass as they called it. Although we were about as 'square' as one could get, we thought it would be a smart move to get some grass, so we would fit in when we reached LA. We asked if John could get us some.

"No problem! I know where we can score." We got into the car and drove several blocks before John told us to pull over. We approached a guy standing on the corner, and after we all greeted each other with this strange new handshake that is accomplished by cupping the hand of the person and interlocking thumbs, signaling that you are hip or cool. In other words, you smoke grass.

The dealer then asked us how much we wanted. We were more concerned with price than anything else, not having any idea about what we were buying. "You guys want a key, a pound, or what?" John smiled, "They just want a lid!" not having any idea what these guys were talking about we agreed. The dealer placed a sheet of newspaper down on the sidewalk. He then placed a coffee can on the paper, taking out a large handful of grass from a bag, he placed some on the top of the can. When the pile became too large for the can's top and it could no longer hold anymore, the measurement was complete. We now had one lid of grass. Something else we also learned that day was that the hippies not only had a secret handshake, but they also spoke their own language. It was based on the use of one main word, 'MAN'. Let me try to explain by a simple example. When we were introduced to John's street contact, he spoke to us in this new language. The conversation went something like this: 'Man, (me) just watch out for the man (Police) man(me). If the man (Police) gets you man(me) man (Oh boy) you're in big trouble man (oh boy)'. Anyway, I hope you get the Idea. Armed with this new information we decided it was time to say goodbye to John and head on down to LA. A large concert was going on over the next few days at a place called Newport. All the towns in the area had their population better than tripled just in the last few days, and it was still growing as we headed on our way.

Chapter 64 *Santa Monica and Newport*

We both smiled as we pulled into Newport. Young people were everywhere. Kids thumbing rides, which at that time was a major method of transportation. If you didn't own a car you just hitchhiked your way around. I guess some bad things happened from time to time but I can't recall ever worrying about the danger involved in hitchhiking. This was starting to look more like what the two of us had been drawn to California for. After finding a place to park, we started to ask around trying to figure out where we could stay. Due to the concert every hotel was totally full.

One group of kids we talked to suggested we check out the beach. It seems that at night it was legal to camp there as long as you got off the beach before they opened to the public in the morning. Because of the large crowds converging on the area, it appeared that our only option was to walk out on the beach and check it out.

The first thing we noticed was this group of around twelve people. They were setting up camp next to this crazy painted Volkswagen bus. We introduced ourselves and after a bit of casual small talk they invited us to set up our camp by them.

Odd when I think back, neither my partner or I had any interest in that concert. We could hear the music off in the distance but basically paid no attention beyond that. I realize now that this was the happening that the two of us had traveled all the way across the country to be a part of. Oh well, funny how life can be.

What turned out to be even odder was the fact that the fella who owned this Volkswagen bus was performing at the concert. He left camp saying he would be back later that night. We questioned some of the people that remained with us. It seemed that this guy was collecting royalties for one song he had recorded. The music had something to do with cocaine in your brain or something like that. He had purchased the bus, and all kinds of gear including scuba tanks and fishing equipment and anything else you could possibly need and started up this traveling company.

The bunch was living in the true manner of a communal lifestyle. Girls would sleep with a different guy every other night or so in some kind of pre-determined arrangement. Everyone worked to do something to help out the entire group. And yes, there was such a thing as free love, 'sorta.

That night when the leader of our new group returned, I decided to offer the bunch the grass we had gotten in San Francisco. I had stuffed it inside a pillow thinking no one would ever think to look there. We all had a good time sitting by the fire, singing some songs and telling stories. I desperately tried to convince this one girl to break off her arrangement for one night before I had to move on, but she would have no part of that suggestion. She told us we would have to stay and become a part of the company for that to happen.

We were both on short time by the time we had gotten to California. We knew we would have to start to make our way home in order to be back in time to report to Whitehall to be shipped out and begin our enlistment. Oh, well.

I must tell you that we had little interest in the grass we had purchased. Beer or wine just seemed like more our style, but the grass did make the people we were with feel more comfortable with us. The fella that had been performing at the concert had finally returned to the camp. He told us that someone had given him some stuff that had never been on the coast before.

He put this stuff in a pipe and told us to only take one puff. Thinking that I really didn't want any but being that we were his guests, and this was supposed to be something special, I figured that one puff couldn't hurt. When I drew on the pipe I instantly noticed this sickening, sweet taste. There was a strong smell of some kind of perfume that surrounded the campfire. Next thing I remember was that a bunch of us started walking down the beach. This one guy kept telling us over and over "Be careful man, don't step on the turtle's man"! I had no Idea what the hell he was talking about. There were no turtles anywhere to be seen.

I can only guess that possibly nesting sea turtles' eggs were hatching, but none of us ever saw any. After a while his constant statements about the turtles started to make us laugh so we all started to repeat to everyone we met the same warning.

The beach was beautiful that night. As the waves rolled in they churned up sand causing it to glow with a blue phosphorescence. Scooping up sand in my hands I noticed that it also appeared to be electrically charged, giving off bright blue sparks. At least I think that's what I saw. Somewhere far down the beach someone was beating on what I can only guess was a fifty-gallon metal drum. The beat never changed. It seemed to keep a strange cadence of one beat a second or so. This repeating drum could be heard the entire night. I started to wonder who the heck would spend an entire night just doing that.

Finally, the noise started to get to me, so turning to one of the guys we were with I asked him, "What's that drumming all about?" "It's time, man, time!" he answered. Its nuts, man, nuts, I thought to myself, not having any idea what the hell he was talking about. It seemed to me that most of these people were crazy.

Oddly enough a band called The Chambers Brothers would record a song that ran almost twelve minutes long which was unique in itself. The beginning of the recording was the annoying tapping like the drum we heard all night long on that California beach. The song title was 'Time has Come Today'.
Now I understand, "It's time, man, time."

As the sun started to rise it was time for the night people to leave the public beaches. We packed up our stuff into the car, nodded our goodbyes to the traveling company and headed for the road. We needed to find some place to get something to eat, also we were both hoping to find some kind of new adventure.

The town of Santa Monica seemed to fit the bill. A large pier and lots of people hanging around the beach areas, probably more than usual due to the concert. We just started casually talking to people, not really having any kind of plan. When we mentioned that we wanted to get something to eat, one guy pointed to the large gazebo by the beach entrance. "The mission brings food there twice a day. It's good food and it's free." Well we had nothing better to do for the day and with all the people walking around we were kinda hoping we might meet some girls. We sorta made friends with the guy that we were talking with figuring he could show us around town a bit. This gazebo turned out to be one very strange place indeed. There was a good crowd of people hanging around as we walked over. The guys from the mission were due to arrive shortly with the afternoon meals.

The first thing we noticed was a girl dressed up like an Indian on the roof. She was dressed in buckskins, complete with feather and painted face, lying on her back looking up at the sky whistling what seemed to be an almost endless variety of bird calls. I was beginning to feel like we had just landed on another planet.

I've never seen so many odd people all gathered together in one place at the same time. My partner needed to use the bathroom which was by the pier. I stayed by the gazebo with our new-found friend. He introduced me to several of the locals he knew from the area. They were all waiting around for the food to arrive, and at the same time asking each other who had stuff to get high. This was when the guy I had befriended pointed to a fella across from us. "Give him a buck and he will play you a song. He can play anything you want to hear"! I wasn't really interested in hearing any songs from this guy, but at the same time I didn't want to seem like some kind of outsider to this group of crazies. I waved him over and he held out a painted tambourine in front of me. "W-what d-do y-you want to hear?" he stuttered as he asked.

Pulling some song off the top of my head I gave him my request, dropping the dollar into his tambourine. That's when the craziest thing happened. He started smacking the side of his leg with the tambourine. Nothing that even came close to any kind of music could be heard in the clatter he was making. At first, I felt a little pissed about this deal but soon enough I started to feel sorry for this poor devil. As my partner returned from the bathroom I couldn't wait to have him request a song. We told him to drop a dollar in that guy's painted tambourine and tell him what song he wanted to hear. After a bit of coaxing he finally placed his order. I could barely keep a straight face as the guy started to smack his green painted instrument up against his leg.

My partner's face dropped, and I quickly reached to grasp his arm before he lunged at this poor fella. Like me, it took a little time for him to see the humor in the situation. He finally started to laugh and clap his hands together. Our happy musician seemed very pleased in our reaction to his music. Whatever the deal was with that guy, we all had a good laugh.

That was when we noticed that there was something strange going on over by the pier. A blue and white school bus had pulled up with a group of around ten people on board. They all quickly exited the bus and started running around by the pier. When I asked what was going on I was told it was the professor and some of his students selling acid. It seems that a professor named Timothy Leary and some of his students had driven a bus down from Berkeley College in order to distribute LSD around the Santa Monica area. I assume they chose the pier because of the large numbers of people that frequently loitered there.

Our curiosity got the best of us, so we decided to take a closer look at what this was all about and what this stuff they were selling looked like. As we got closer, one of the students approached us with something that looked like a strip of candy dots. If you're anywhere close to my age you should remember this type of candy. This LSD thing was totally new to me at the time. I had no idea what these students were talking about when they asked if we wanted to take a trip, but we both decided not to get involved.

The group didn't remain in the area long, maybe twenty minutes at best. By using a hit and run method they wouldn't draw too much attention to themselves. This bus trip was not their first visit to the pier. Many of the people there were waiting for the bus to arrive. If I'm not mistaken, LSD was actually not illegal. But as the popularity of psychedelics grew with our generation, so did the laws to prevent it from being distributed.

Something else was happening while we were observing the activity on the pier. We had taken a cassette radio that some call a boom box along with us on the road trip. When my partner and I decided to check out the pier we left it in the care of our new friend. Upon our return he was nowhere to be seen. We asked several people that were hanging around the area if they had seen where our friend went, and quickly realized the possibility that we had been ripped off.

The first thing both of us did was to grab our guns from under the seat of the car. It was strange but at that time we worried more about the lid of grass that we kept hidden inside of one of our pillows than the loaded guns under the seat in the car. I guess as someone recently said to me, "In our young days we believed we were bullet proof." Slipping our guns into our belts, we fanned out under the columns that supported the pier not wanting to really cause any harm to this guy. We just wanted to make sure he didn't try anything if we caught up with him. Our anger had definitely gotten the best of us and we made sure every one of his friends knew we were both packing pistols.

That was a dumb move because that guy wouldn't come within a mile of the pier once he knew he might be at risk of getting shot. Needless to say, we never caught up with him. The boombox was gone. We both decided we had seen enough of California. It was time to start the long return trip home.

Chapter 65 *Arizona Nights*

Somewhere outside of Phoenix the Corvair suddenly started to sputter, and a red light appeared on the dash. We knew right away what the car was up to, 'vapor lock'. The desert air temperature was well over a hundred and five degrees. Even though we were driving with the top down the heat in the car was still unbearable.

So, as the car slowly rolled to a stop on the shoulder we made the decision that we had driven long enough. It was time for us to call it a day, so as we climbed out of the car we started looking about for a suitable place to set up camp. This desert road seemed to be almost completely voided of traffic. It felt like we were standing at the end of the world. The ground under our feet was hard like concrete, with landscape so flat it gave the appearance that it just went on forever. The desert appeared to be totally lifeless. We concluded that nothing could possibly live in such a barren place except for the cactus. These giant, forked plants reminded us of some old western movie as they stood twelve to fifteen feet tall casting their towering shadows across this uninhabitable wasteland.

We decided we'd just throw our sleeping bags down on the desert floor. Sleeping under the stars in a vast open place like this should be a pretty cool thing to do. As the night sky finally started to collide with the day, these two weary travelers finished off a six pack of beer and a few hot dogs before crawling into our cocoons for the night. As we glanced up at the evening sky, I must tell you it was one of the most incredible sights you could ever imagine. Billions of stars sparkled like diamonds in the blue-black desert sky. Shooting stars blasted their way across this vast heavenly dome that seemed to cover us like a giant umbrella. The heat of the day was quickly leaving, and the cool night air caused us to zip up our bags before we slipped off into sleep. Fatigued from spending the day driving through extreme heat of the Arizona desert, the two of us slept well into late morning before we awoke. The heat was once again starting to climb and we both were becoming uncomfortable in our insulated sleeping bags. As I started to sit up something instantly caught my attention.

The ground around us had gone through some kind of an incredible transformation while the two of us soundly slept throughout the night. As it turns out, during the day the desert is indeed a lifeless place, but as night's sky covers the land and the cooling air moistens the sun baked floor, this seemingly barren terrain becomes alive with life.

Tracks from all kinds of crawling creatures had left their telltale signs around our sleeping bags. Rats, giant spiders, scorpions and what bothered me most, the 'S' shaped trail which I recognized instantly as one made by a Sidewinder Rattlesnake. All these creatures had been crawling all around and over us during the night. I started calling over to my partner to wake up, not knowing if any of these critters had gotten into our bags. Never have I moved so fast as I did that day. We both got a good distance away from our sleeping bags before we carefully attempted to check them for intruders.

Luckily, none of these creatures decided to share quarters with us that night. After checking our bags really well and shaking out our clothes, we climbed back into our car. The cool night air had taken care of the Corvair's vapor lock, and it started up without a problem. We were once again on our way.

So, let this story be a reminder, if you ever get the chance and decide that sleeping in the desert seems like a good idea, be careful, because there are many things out there that go bump in the night.

Chapter 66 *Willow Creek*

Just as all things eventually come to an end, so did our road trip. Time was fast approaching for us to report for our deployment. This journey had been somewhat of a wild ride for the two of us. Sad that things you enjoy seem to pass by so quickly, leaving behind only the memory of their dusty tracks, like those of the Sidewinder that moved across the desert in the darkness of night. Only his wispy marks remain in the sand to let you know he ever existed at all.

We still had a week or so to recuperate after we returned home to Willow Creek before we would once again say goodbye to our parents and friends and head to New York City.

They had given us a list of personal belongings to bring, toiletries and such. Each of us carried these small bags at our sides. The next step in our deployment process was a second physical before they shipped us out. This is when things suddenly took a drastic turn for me. Before I continue I must take you back to my sophomore year in high school. It was football season and we had just finished practice and were heading into the locker room.

I had stopped at the water fountain for a drink when the coach noticed something that stopped him dead in his tracks. It seemed that somehow, I had been injured, and the back of my jersey was totally red with blood. At the time I felt nothing and became very perplexed when they started to cut the jersey and shoulder pads off my back. The coach thought maybe somehow glass had gotten under my jersey and it had sliced my back to ribbons. After finally removing all my gear, they were not able to find any cuts. Instead, what they observed was all the skin on my entire back was basically gone. Concerned that it might actually be a really bad case of something called Impetigo which can be highly contagious, I was sent home with orders to see a doctor before I returned to practice. The coaches had the entire locker room disinfected in my absence.

The first doctor I went to see gave me some type of antibiotic cream, which after a week of use gave no relief for my problem.

The decision was made to send me to a skin specialist. A biopsy of my back was taken, and after a good deal of research the doctors finally discovered my problem. My troubles were genetic in nature. I was an adopted child, and apparently one of my birth parents had passed along this skin deficiency called Hailey-Hailey disease, or HHD.

The only known treatment at the time was the use of compound steroids. No cure was available and the best I could hope for was a remission.

Sadly, this put an abrupt end to sports, particularly my participation in playing high school football.

So here we both stood three years later in a lineup at White Hall, our personal bag in hand as the doctors checked us one last time. We were once again told to strip down to our shorts and wait our turn to be examined. As fate would have it, I was having a bloom of this wretched condition just at that very moment. The doctors asked me what was with my back. "Awe, it's nothing" I replied. "Just an inherited skin condition that kicks up every now and then." That was when they asked me for the name of the condition. "HHD" I told them. With that I was told to take a seat and the doctor went back into an office.

It seemed like about a half hour passed before several doctors emerged from the room. One of these doctors was holding a medical journal. He looked down at a page in the book and read the words 'aggravated by stress and high humidity!' "Son, where did you think you were going?" They looked at each other, then back at me. "Have a nice life son! you're out of here!" I stood there in shock, stunned, not knowing what to say. Thoughts started to spin through my memory. "What are you going to do with your life? You have to get some kind of occupation!" All the family pressures that had been lifted the day we enlisted came rushing back into my head. Both my partner and I had feared what our futures might hold, but at least we had some kind of direction.

We'd spent the entire summer with a devil may care disposition traveling around the country knowing we were about to enter into what we believed would be a life changing event.

Suddenly my partner entered the room. "Well Buddy, this is it" he said. "I'm going home" I said back to him, still reeling from what I'd just been told. He looked at me totally confused. For some reason words were just not finding their way out of my mouth. That was the last time I would ever see him.

He eventually would send me a few letters. The first was from Thailand where he met a girl and was living off base. He seemed somewhat happy with this arrangement, saying it was just like a regular civilian job.

After that he returned to the States and met another girl with a couple of kids. I heard that they were married and that was the last I ever heard about him. After I returned home I was lost, feeling like I had let down my friend, my family and my country. Suddenly my entire future had been flipped upside down on its ear.

The military would send me two reclassification slips before finally sending me an honorable discharge.

Being that my original plan was to go into aviation and I still had no real idea what I wanted to do with my life, I enrolled into a school for aviation mechanics. During this time, I had been dating a girl from Willow Creek High School. We decided that after her graduation the two of us would get married. We did. Afterwards, we moved into an apartment in a town not far from Willow Creek.

This was to be the beginning of the next chapter in my life. But this my friends would be after Willow Creek, and that's another story...

Epilogue: *Return to Willow Creek*

After I had finished compiling the words which I have placed on these pages, I felt a desire to return to Willow Creek in an attempt to recapture in photographs some of the places I had written about. Silly me! Although my memories had all been safely stored away in that old dusty closet place in my mind, I have become aware that time has played a devilish game and completely changed many of the places as I remembered them from my youth. The fields we used to slay-ride on are now a heavily wooded development of expensive homes. It is impossible to even tell there was ever a hill there at all.

Same can be said for almost all the places which I have mentioned. Time has erased the Willow Creek of my childhood. It can now only be found in the distant memories of those of you who spent their early days growing up during that special time so long ago.

I did manage to take a photo of the old Erie Railroad Station. It has been beautifully restored as an historical memory of days gone by. I did find it to be somewhat better in appearance than it was back in the days when I was a youngster. One other photo I was able to get was the home of the two nice ladies who baked us cookies after our day of tunnel-crawling. Their home the Hermitage, was taken over by the state just as they had willed it to happen.

I had decided to end my visit at the house where I was raised. The yard is now fenced, and the house has been re-sided in a new color. The front entrance has been reconstructed with pillars giving it a very different look. The one thing that still remains as it was when I was young is my bedroom window. As I looked up at the roof by the window, a smile suddenly came to my face. I could still see the cattails drying in the sun and a young boy crawling out for a night of mischief. I can't help but wonder who uses that room today? Could it be that this person will also find adventure just outside that bedroom window? I can only hope they will. I wish all who read this book find mostly good memories from a time long past but not forgotten.

Alan Sauer...

Made in the USA
Middletown, DE
30 August 2020